DESIGNER Amigurumi

A Cosmopolitan Collection of Crochet Creations from Talented Designers

DILEK YILDIRIM · KATERINA NIKOLAIDAU · KRISTI TULLUS · KRISTINA TURNER

MARI-LIIS LILLE · SANDRINE DEVEZE · SOLEDAD IGLESIAS SILVA

TATYANA KOROBKOVA · TINE NIELSEN

Tuva Publishing
www.tuvapublishing.com

Address Merkez Mah. Cavusbasi Cad. No:71
Cekmekoy - Istanbul 34782 / Turkey
Tel: +9 0216 642 62 62

Designer Amigurumi

First Print 2018 / February

All Global Copyrights Belong To
Tuva Tekstil ve Yayıncılık Ltd.

Content Crochet

Editor in Chief Ayhan DEMİRPEHLİVAN
Project Editor Kader DEMİRPEHLİVAN
Designers Dilek YILDIRIM, Katerina NIKOLAIDAU,
Kristi TULLUS, Kristina TURNER, Mari-Liis LILLE, Sandrine DEVEZE,
Soledad Iglesias SILVA, Tatyana KOROBKOVA, Tine NIELSEN
Technical Editors Leyla ARAS, Büşra ESER
Graphic Designers Ömer ALP, Abdullah BAYRAKÇI, Tarık TOKGÖZ
Photography Tuva Publishing
Crochet Tech Editors Wendi CUSINS, Helen GAINSFORD

ISBN 978-605-9192-35-4

CONTENTS

Project Gallery

Page 28

Page 36

Page 42

Page 48

Page 54

Page 60

Page 66

Page 72

Page 78

Page 84

Page 90

Page 98

Page 102

Page 112

Page 120

Page 126

Page 132

Page 138

Introduction

What is Amigurumi?

Have you ever wondered what "Amigurumi" is? And can you even pronounce it? (In English, we say ah-mee-goo-roo-mee). The word itself comes from two Japanese words – one meaning "crocheted (or knitted)" and the other meaning "stuffed toy". Nowadays, amigurumi is not limited to only toys. Just about anything with a solid 3-D shape can be made using the amigurumi technique. In crochet, when one talks about this technique, one is generally referring to a project worked in spiral rounds using single crochet stitches.

Why Designer Amigurumi?

Amigurumi has become very popular these days and there are plenty of books available for this technique. So what makes Designer Amigurumi stand out from the rest?

For starters, we have nine accomplished designers from various countries around the world, each with their own creative flair and unique use of color.

Secondly, we have a wonderful book of eighteen original crochet designs – from delightful dolls (some with accessories) to a whole menagerie of amazing animals. Every one of these charming creations has their own personality and reflect their designer's characteristic style.

And then, we have easy-to-follow written instructions for each design, together with support photographs and illustrations. There is also a section explaining the various special stitches and techniques needed for amigurumi, as well as the embroidery stitches used in the making of the designs.

Also, this book is suitable for every crochet skill level. Some of the designs are beginner-friendly, but even the more advanced patterns can be tackled as a challenge.

Lastly... Nothing is more appreciated than a hand-made gift. Whether it is for a baby shower (remember to use 'baby-safe' products), a child's birthday party or as presents for family members and friends. You can also make healthy toys by using natural fibers, such as cotton, when crocheting the projects.

We hope you have great fun making and creating the sweet dolls and cute animals featured in this book.

Happy crocheting!

Materials We Used

Safety Warning

When making toys for children under the age of three (including babies), be sure to use child-friendly products.

We advise you avoid the following:
> 'Fuzzy' yarns, where the lint can be inhaled or swallowed.
> Glass Eyes or beads, which can shatter or break.
> Small beads and buttons (including some safety eyes) can be chewed off and swallowed or become a choking hazard.

General Safety Tips

1 Make sure each piece of the toy is sewn firmly onto the body.
2 Instead of using Safety Eyes, buttons or beads, you can use crocheted or felt circles, sewn on firmly.
3 You can create features on your toys with simple embroidery stitches.

Note These Safety Warnings also apply when you make toys for pets.

The Yarns

All the designs in this book were made using the DMC Natura Just Cotton family of yarn. We prefer using the cotton yarns when making toys. It is a natural fiber and easy to care for, as it is machine-washable. When we needed 'hairier' bits, we used the DMC Woolly.

Should you want to substitute the yarns used in the patterns with other yarn, please adjust your hook size to get either the correct gauge or 'feel' of the fabric.

 **DMC Natura Just Cotton**

Natura Just Cotton is a yarn made from 100% cotton. It has a matte finish, which makes it lovely to use for crochet. The long fibers give it softness and strength, creating a fabric with good stitch definition.

DMC Natura Medium Just Cotton

The Medium version of Natura Just Cotton is a wonderful worsted weight, 100% cotton yarn. It has a smooth texture and a firm twist, making it very durable and easy to work with.

DMC Natura XL Just Cotton

Natura XL is a super bulky, 100% combed cotton yarn with a matte finish.

 **DMC Natura Yummy**

The Yummy Range of Natura is the same yarn as the Natura Just Cotton, just with 'yummy' colors.

 **DMC Woolly**

Woolly is a light weight yarn made of 100% Merino wool, recognized as the best wool in the world. It is 100% natural and renewable. It is easy to care for (machine-washable) and pleasant to work with.

The Hooks

We love using the Clover Amour Hooks which are ergonomic, comfortable and easy to hold. Each size hook has its own color, making it easy to remember which hook you're using.

Hook Size Conversion Table

Metric	U.S.	UK/Canada
2.25 mm	B-1	13
2.75 mm	C-2	12
3.00 mm	-	11
3.25 mm	D-3	10
3.50 mm	E-4	-
3.75 mm	F-5	9
4.00 mm	G-6	8
4.50 mm	7	7
5.00 mm	H-8	6
5.50 mm	I-9	5
6.00 mm	J-10	4
6.50 mm	K-10 ½	3

The Stuffing

When it comes to stuffing your toys, there are quite a few options available. Whichever stuffing you choose, make sure it is fluffy and does not clump. We used **polyester fiberfill** (also known as polyfill or fiberfill) for the stuffing in all the toys.

Polyester pellets (which are heavier than stuffing) can also be used if you want a bit of weight in your toy. You can also combine polyfill with pellets while stuffing.

Please do NOT use stuffing like rice or beans, which might rot and decay, which could attract creepy crawlies.

The Stitch Markers

Keeping track of the last (or first) stitch while working a crocheted spiral round is important for the stitch counts. Locking stitch markers are the best tool for this as they can be opened and closed easily.

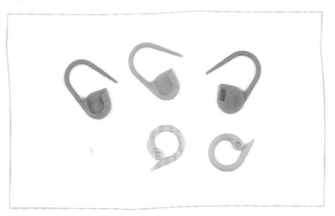

Alternatively, you can use a separate piece of yarn (in another color), a safety pin, or even a paperclip.

The Yarn (Tapestry) Needle

This needle is needed for joining the different crochet pieces together, as well as for weaving in the yarn ends.

Preferably use a blunt-tipped needle which will not split the yarn. You could also use a bent-tip tapestry needle. Make sure the eye of the needle is large enough for the yarn you're using. We also find that the metal needles work much better with amigurumi than the plastic needles.

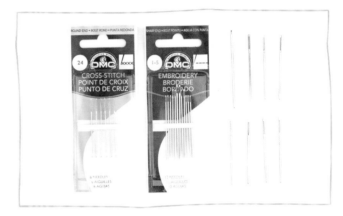

The Safety Eyes (& Noses)

Eyes and facial features give the toys character. Using safety eyes and a safety nose is a quick way of achieving this. Generally the eye or nose is attached to a ribbed shank, which is inserted through the fabric. A locking washer is applied to the shank, keeping the eye (or nose) in place. These eyes and noses can be made from plastic, glass or acrylic, and come in a range of shapes, sizes and colors. Once they are attached, it is almost impossible to pull them out. Before using them, please read the Safety Warning.

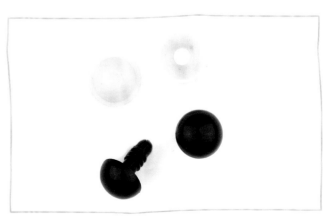

Sometimes it is easy enough to attach these eyes using only your fingers. For those who find it difficult, there is a safety eye insertion tool which can be used to attach the washers.

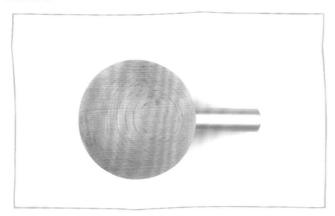

The Embroidery Floss / Perle Cotton Thread

DMC has wide range of Perle or Stranded cottons, which can be used to embellish your toys. You can use them to embroider facial features, or enhance their overall appearance by adding cross-stitch motifs or embroidered flowers.

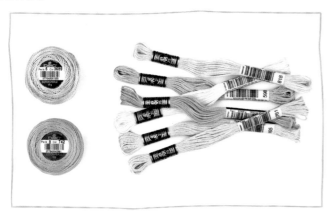

The Felts & Fabrics

Using small pieces of felt or fabric is also a great way to embellish your toys. They can be used as appliqué patches or as clothing accessories, like scarves.

The Sewing Needle & Thread

When we need to apply appliqué (either crocheted of fabric), we use a needle and thread. Use a good quality thread to sew the pieces on securely.

The Other Materials

Small Scissors
Straight Pins (with large heads)
Pompom makers
Buttons
Cosmetic blusher for cheeks

General Information For Making Amigurumi

Choosing the Hook

Use a hook which is a size or two smaller than what is recommended on the yarn label. The fabric created should be tight enough so that the stuffing does not show through the stitches.

Right Side vs Wrong Side of the Fabric

It is important to be able to distinguish between the 'right' (front) and 'wrong' (back) side of the crocheted fabric.

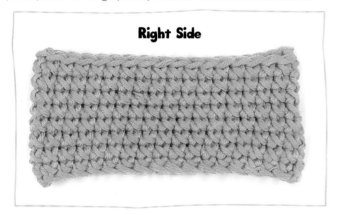
Right Side

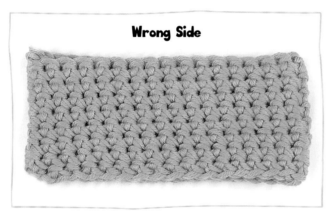
Wrong Side

When working in a spiral or joined round, the right side of the fabric is always facing you. Working in rows or turned rounds, it will alternate between 'right' and 'wrong' side.

Single Crochet Rows

Working in a Spiral

Most of the amigurumi pieces are worked in a continuous spiral to create the dimensional shapes needed. Working in a spiral means that at the end of a round, you do not join (or close) with a slip stitch into the first stitch of the round. When you get to the end of the round, you start the next round by just working a stitch into the next stitch (which is the first stitch of the previous round).

Using Stitch Markers

When working in a spiral, it is important to keep track of the round you are working on as well as the stitch count for the round. To do this, use a stitch marker placed in the last stitch of the round. Some people prefer marking the first stitch of the round. Whichever you choose, keep consistent throughout project piece.

Hint Count your stitches after each round (and row) to ensure you have the correct stitch count.

Working in Joined (Closed) Rounds

Some parts of an amigurumi pattern might have 'joined rounds'. This is where, at the end of the round, you join with a slip stitch in the first stitch of the round. The next round starts with a number of chain stitches (based on height of the stitches used), and then you continue working stitches for the next round.

Note Do not turn at the end of each joined round, unless instructed to do so.

Working in Rows

For some accessories or patches for your amigurumi, you will need to work in rows. Each row starts by turning the piece and working some chain stitches (known as the 'turning chain'). The number of chain stitches worked is based on the height of the stitches used.

Stuffing

The pieces of the toys need to get stuffed to hold their correct shape. Some pieces only need a "light stuffing" – just enough stuffing to hold the shape. When the pattern calls for a piece to be "stuffed firmly", you need to stuff it as tight as you can, and then add a bit more. The back of your crochet hook or a plastic chopstick can be used as a stuffing tool to help you spread the stuffing into every little nook and cranny.

Tip Stuff the pieces of your toy as you're making them.

Adapting The Design

There are many ways you can make your amigurumi toy unique.

Size By choosing a different weight yarn, you can make your toys either bigger (using thicker yarn) or smaller (using thinner yarn or thread). Remember to change your hook size too.

Colors This is the easiest way to make your toy unique. Select colors to match décor or personal preference.

Characteristics Changing the facial features of toys, gives them a whole new character. By adding (or removing) embellishments to the overall toy, can change the whole look of it.

Eyes Just by changing the size or color of the eyes, can create a totally different facial expression. Instead of using safety eyes, you can use buttons or beads for eyes. If there is a safety concern, you can sew on small bits of felt for eyes or embroider the features.

Blusher Adding some color to the cheeks, is another way of changing the character of toys. You can apply cosmetic pink blusher or eyeshadow using a small makeup brush or cotton bud (Q-Tip). Another way to do this, is to rub a red pencil on a piece of fabric, pressing down hard. Then rub the 'red' fabric on the cheeks as blusher.

Applique patches Whether they are crocheted, fabric or felt (or a combination of these), adding appliqué patches to your doll is a great way to make your toys distinctive. They can be facial features, such as eyes, noses, mouths, cheeks, and maybe even ears. You can also make novelty appliqué patches to use as embellishment on the toys. For example – flowers on a dress, eye-patch for a pirate, overall patch for a farmer. The creativity becomes endless.

Embroidery By adding embroidery stitches to the face, the character of the toy can change. Whether you use plain embroidery stitches (straight stitch, back stitch, etc.) or fancy ones (satin stitch, French knot, bullion stitch, etc.), your toy will take on a personality of its own. You can also use the cross-stitch technique to create a unique look.

Note Embroider all facial features to make a child-safe toy.

Crochet surface stitches This technique is worked on a finished crochet fabric. It can be used for outlines, emphasis or decoration.

Pompoms These little balls are very versatile. Making them in different sizes, you can use them as bunny tails, or to decorate the toy. A great tool to use is the Clover pompom maker, which comes in various sizes. You can also make them using other methods, like wrapping around a fork or piece of cardboard.

Adding accessories To create your one-of-a-kind toy, you can add various decorations to them. Colored buttons can be used in a variety of ways to spice things up. Using small ribbons and bows can feminize dolls. Attaching a small bunch of flowers or small basket to a doll's hand, tells a new story.

However you choose to give your toy character, each one ends up being unique!

Crochet Terminology

This book uses US crochet terminology.

Basic conversion chart

US	UK
slip stitch (sl st)	slip stitch (sl st)
chain (ch)	chain (ch)
single crochet (sc)	double crochet (dc)
double crochet (dc)	treble crochet (tr)
half-double crochet (hdc)	half treble (htr)
treble (triple) crochet (tr)	double treble (dtr)

Abbreviations Of The Basic Stitches

ch	Chain Stitch
sl st	Slip Stitch
sc	Single Crochet Stitch
hdc	Half-Double Crochet Stitch
dc	Double Crochet Stitch
tr	Treble (or Triple) Crochet Stitch

Concise Action Terms

dec	Decrease (reduce by one or more stitches)
inc	Increase (add one or more stitches)
join	Join two stitches together, usually with a slip stitch. (Either to complete the end of a round or when introducing a new ball or color of yarn)
rep	Repeat (the previous marked instructions)
turn	Turn your crochet piece so you can work back for the next row/round
yo	Yarn over the hook. (Either to pull up a loop or to draw through the loops on hook)

Standard Symbols Used in Patterns

[ ]	Work instructions within brackets as many times as directed
( )	Work instructions within parentheses in same stitch or space indicated
*	Repeat the instructions following the single asterisk as directed
**	1) Repeat instructions between asterisks as many times as directed; or 2) Repeat from a given set of instructions

Crochet Basics

Slip Knot

Almost every crochet project starts with a slip knot on the hook. This is not mentioned in any pattern – it is assumed.

To make a slip knot, form a loop with your yarn (the tail end hanging behind your loop); insert the hook through the loop, and pick up the ball end of the yarn. Draw yarn through loop. Keeping loop on hook, gently tug the tail end to tighten the knot. Tugging the ball end tightens the loop.

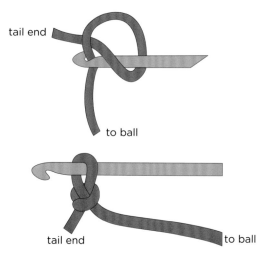

Yarn Over (yo)

This is a common practice, especially with the taller stitches.

With a loop on your hook, wrap the yarn (attached to the ball) from back to front around the shaft of your hook.

Chain Stitch (ch)

The chain stitch is the foundation of most crochet projects. The foundation chain is a series of chain stitches in which you work the first row of stitches.

To make a chain stitch, you start with a slip knot (or loop) on the hook. Yarn over and pull the yarn through the loop on your hook (first chain stitch made). For more chain stitches, repeat: Yarn over, pull through loop on hook.

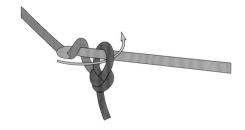

Hint Don't pull the stitches too tight, otherwise they will be difficult to work in.

When counting chain stitches, do not count the slip knot, nor the loop on the hook. Only count the number of 'v's.

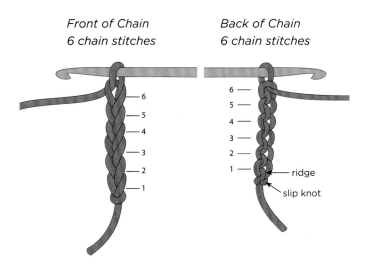

*Front of Chain
6 chain stitches*

*Back of Chain
6 chain stitches*

Slip Stitch (sl st)

Starting with a loop on your hook, insert hook in stitch or space specified and pull up a loop, pulling it through the loop on your hook as well.
The slip stitch is commonly used to attach new yarn and to join rounds.

Attaching a New Color or New Ball of Yarn (or Joining with a Slip Stitch (join with sl st)).

Make a slip knot with the new color (or yarn) and place loop on hook. Insert hook from front to back in the (usually) first stitch (unless specified otherwise). Yarn over and pull loop through stitch and loop on hook (slip stitch made).

Single Crochet (sc)

Starting with a loop on your hook, insert hook in stitch or space specified and draw up a loop (two loops on hook). Yarn over and pull yarn through both the loops on your hook (first sc made).

The height of a single crochet stitch is one chain high.

When working single crochet stitches into a foundation chain, begin the first single crochet in the second chain from the hook. The skipped chain stitch provides the height of the stitch.

At the beginning of a single crochet row or round, start by making one chain stitch (to get the height) and work the first single crochet stitch into first stitch (Note: The one chain stitch is never counted as a single crochet stitch).

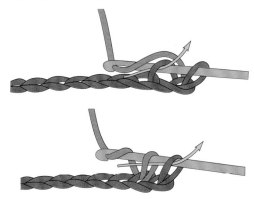

Half-Double Crochet (hdc)

Starting with a loop on your hook, yarn over hook before inserting hook in stitch or space specified and draw up a loop (three loops on hook). Yarn over and pull yarn through all three loops (first hdc made).

The height of a half-double crochet stitch is two chains high.

When working half-double crochet stitches into a foundation chain, begin the first stitch in the third chain from the hook. The two skipped chains provide the height. When starting a row or round with a half-double crochet stitch, make two chain stitches and work in the first stitch (Note: The two chain stitches are never counted as a half-double stitch).

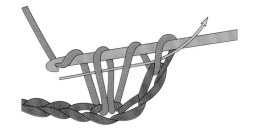

Double Crochet (dc)

Starting with a loop on your hook, yarn over hook before inserting hook in stitch or space specified and draw up a loop (three loops on hook). Yarn over and pull yarn through two loops (two loops remain on hook). Yarn over and pull yarn through remaining two loops on hook (first dc made).

The height of a double crochet stitch is three chains high.

When working double crochet stitches into a foundation chain, begin the first stitch in the fourth chain from the hook.

The three skipped chains count as the first double crochet stitch. When starting a row or round with a double crochet stitch, make three chain stitches (which count as the first double crochet), skip the first stitch (under the chains) and work a double crochet in the next (second) stitch. On the following row or round, when you work in the 'made' stitch, you will be working in the top chain (3rd chain stitch of the three chains).

Treble (Or Triple) Crochet (tr)

Starting with a loop on your hook, yarn over hook twice before inserting hook in stitch or space specified and draw up a loop (four loops on hook). Yarn over and pull yarn through two loops (three loops remain on hook). Again, make a yarn over and pull yarn through two loops (two loops remain on hook). Once more, yarn over and pull through remaining two loops (first tr made).

The height of a treble crochet stitch is four chains high. When working treble crochet stitches into a foundation chain, begin the first stitch in the fifth chain from the hook. The four skipped chains count as the first treble crochet stitch. When starting a row or round with a treble crochet stitch, make four chain stitches (which count as the first treble crochet), skip the first stitch (under the chains) and work a treble crochet in the next (second) stitch. On the following row or round, when you work in the 'made' stitch, you will be working in the top chain (4th chain stitch of the four chains).w

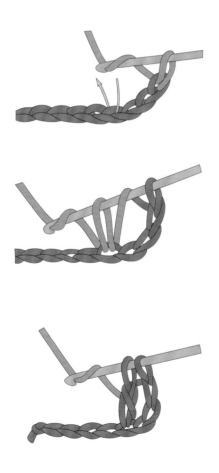

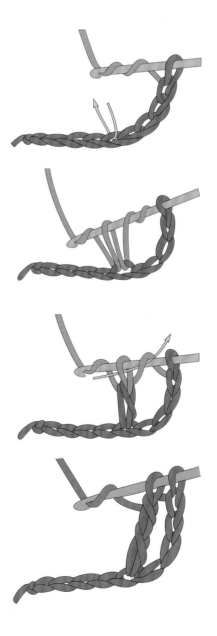

Special Stitches Used in Amigurumi

Invisible Single Crochet Decrease (sc-dec)

Insert the hook into the front loops of the next 2 stitches (3 loops on hook).

Yarn over and draw through first two loops on hook (2 loops remain on hook).

Yarn over and draw through both loops on hook (sc-dec made).

Note If you prefer, you can use the normal single crochet decrease stitch.

Single Crochet Decrease - "normal decrease" (sc2tog)

Insert hook in next stitch and pull up a loop, (two loops on hook).

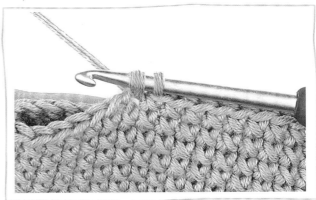

Insert hook in next stitch and pull up a loop (three loops on hook).

Yarn over, draw through all three loops on hook.

Hint Use the invisible decrease (sc-dec) when working in the continuous spiral rounds and use the normal decrease (sc2tog) when working in rows.

Single Crochet Increase (inc)

Work 2 single crochet stitches in the same stitch indicated.

Single Crochet Double Increase (inc3)

Work 3 single crochet stitches in the same stitch indicated.

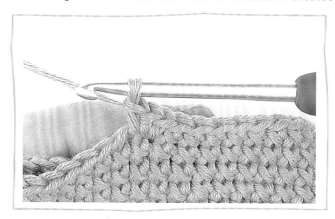

Crochet Techniques For Amigurumi

Back Ridge Of Foundation Chain

The back ridge (also called back bumps or back bars) is found on wrong side of the foundation chain. It consists of single loops behind the 'v-loops'. To work in the back ridge, one inserts the hook from front to back through the back ridge loop to pull up the yarn. Working in the Back Ridge gives a neater finish to projects.

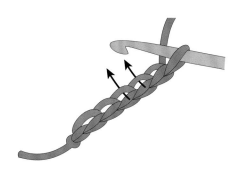

Changing Colors / Attaching New Yarn

With the current color, work the last stitch before the color change up to the last step of the stitch. Using the new color, yarn over hook, pull new color through remaining loops on hook.

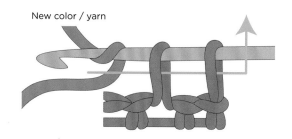

New color / yarn

Close The Opening

Working in the stitches of the last round, insert the yarn needle from back to front through the front loop of each stitch around. Gently pull the yarn to tighten the hole. Once the opening is closed, secure the yarn. Insert the needle back through the center of the ring and taking care (squashing the stuffing), bring it out at an inconspicuous place on the piece. Work a few weaving stitches before inserting the needle back through the stuffed piece and out at another point. Cut the yarn close to the piece so that it retracts into the stuffing.

Fasten Off

After the last single crochet stitch is worked, work a slip stitch in the next stitch. Cut the yarn, leaving a tail. With the tail, yarn over and pull the tail through the stitch.

Fitting Safety Eyes / Nose

Choose and mark the positions for the eyes (or nose) on the front of the face. Insert the shank of the eye (or nose) through the fabric from right side to wrong side. (The eye is on the front side, the shank sticks out at the back.) Attach the locking washer onto the shank and push down firmly to lock it tightly. You can use a safety eye insertion tool for doing this.

Front And Back Loops

Every stitch has what looks like 'v's on the top. There are two loops that make up the 'v'. The front loop is the loop closest to you and the back loop is the loop furthest from you. Generally, we work in both loops – under both the front and back loops. Working in either the front or back loops only, creates a decorative ridge (made up of the unworked loops).

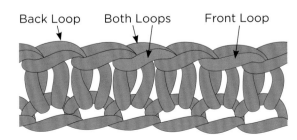

Note Work all stitches under both loops unless otherwise instructed.

Invisible Join

After the last stitch is worked (do not slip stitch in next stitch), cut the yarn leaving a tail and pull the tail through the last stitch. Using the tail and a yarn needle, skip the next stitch and insert the needle under both loops of the following stitch. Then insert the needle into the back loop of the last stitch made (the same stitch where the tail came through) and also through the horizontal loop of the stitch (for stability). Gently tug the yarn so that it looks like a "stitch" and matches the others. Secure this "stitch" and weave in the tail.

Join With SC (Single Crochet Standing Stitch)

With a slip knot on hook, insert hook into stitch or space specified and pull up a loop (two loops on hook). Yarn over and pull through both loops on hook (first single crochet made).

Join with Slip Knot

Using the yarn, make a slip knot. Do not insert your hook through loop. Insert your hook in the stitch or space indicated and place the loop of the slip knot on the loop. Gently pull the loop through the stitch, keeping the knot at the back. Continue with the pattern.

Magic Ring (Or Adjustable Ring)

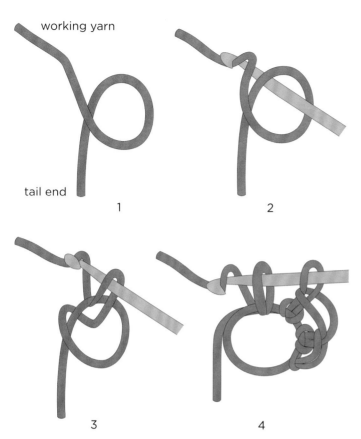

1 Form a loop with the yarn, keeping the tail end of the yarn behind the working yarn (the yarn attached to the ball).

2 Insert the hook through the loop (from front to back), and pull the working yarn through the loop (from back to front). Do not tighten up the loop.

3 Using the working yarn, make a chain stitch (to secure the ring). This chain stitch does NOT count as first stitch.

4 Work the required stitches into the ring (over the tail strand). When all the stitches are done, gently tug the tail end to close the ring, before joining the round (if specified). Remember, make sure this tail is firmly secured before weaving in the end.

Note If you prefer, you can use any type of "ring" to start your project (or start with ch-2, and working the first round in the second chain from hook). The advantage of using the adjustable Magic Ring, is that when it is tightened, it closes the hole completely.

Tip Secure your Magic Ring after the first few rounds and before you start stuffing.

Weaving in Yarn Tails

Thread the tail onto a yarn needle. Starting close to where the tail begins, preferably working on the wrong side, weave the tail through the back of stitches (preferably of the same color) to hide the yarn. When done, trim the tail close to the fabric.

For weaving in ends on an already stuffed pieces, you can secure the yarn close to the piece and then insert the needle through the stuffing and out the other side. If you want, you can do this a few times. When done, cut the yarn close to the toy and let the end disappear inside.

Jointed Toys

Instead of plastic doll joints, you can use cotter pin joints, buttons and thread, or even just thread.

Using Plastic Doll Joints

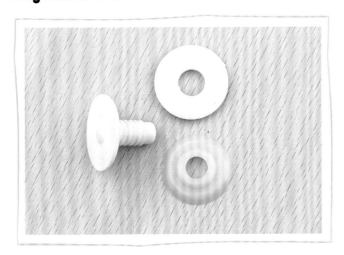

Each joint consists of three pieces – a disc with a stem, a washer, and a fastener.

The disc with a stem in inserted from inside the limbs, with the stem protruding through the fabric.

The stem is then inserted into the Body. First place the washer over the stem, and then the fastener.

Making Button and Thread Joints

The thread used should be very strong and able to withstand a lot of tension. Cotton embroidery floss, nylon sewing thread (doubled or tripled) or even fishing line, works really well.

Cut a length of strong thread/yarn and draw through holes in button

Place the button inside the limb and using yarn needle, draw the doubled thread through the fabric.

Insert the yarn needle with doubled thread into the Body. Place another button inside the body and draw each thread through a different hole in the button. Knot the thread tails together.

Other Crochet Stitches & Techniques Used in the Book

Popcorn Stitch (Cheeky Bird)

Popcorns add texture to a project as they really 'pop' out. They are made by working a number of stitches into the same stitch or space. The working loop is then dropped from the hook and the hook inserted in the first stitch of the group. The loop is put back on the hook and drawn through the stitch.

Tapestry Crochet (Heart Cat)

This technique of crochet color-work consists of working with two or more colors at the same time. The unused colors are carried along by working over the strands with the current color, until they are needed.

Note When the unused colors are stranded at the back of the work, the technique is then called Fair Isle. Dropping the unused yarn and then picking it up when needed, is referred to as Intarsia – another color-work technique.

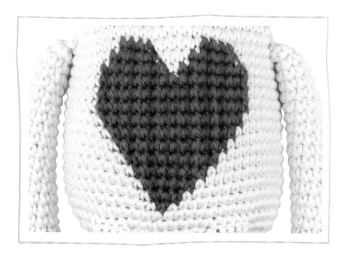

Shell Stitch (Happy Girl)

This common crochet stitch can also be called the Fan Stitch. A number of long stitches are worked into the same stitch of space, creating a semi-circle or arc of stitches. They are often used as borders or edgings in projects.

Loop Stitch (Leo The Lion)

This stitch is wonderful when used as an accent on toys, Afghans and clothing. It is made by wrapping the yarn around your finger to create the loop.

Embriodery Stitches

When embroidering on crochet, it is recommended to insert the needle through the yarn of the stitch and not through the 'holes' between the stitches. This makes it easier to control the placement of the embroidery thread.

Back Stitch

Bring threaded needle up from wrong to right side of fabric (#1). Insert needle back down a bit before (#2) and bring it out a bit ahead (#3) on the desired outline. Insert the needle back down through the same hole (#1) and bring it out a bit ahead again. Repeat along the desired outline.

Bullion Stitch

Bring threaded needle up from wrong to right side of fabric at the position where you want the knot to start (#1). Insert the needle back into the fabric at the position where you want the knot to end (#2) and back up through the starting point (#1) – without pulling the needle through. Wrap the yarn/thread around tip of needle as many times as needed. Hold the wrapped loops as you gently pull the needle through the fabric and loops to form the Knot. Insert the needle back through the fabric to the wrong side.

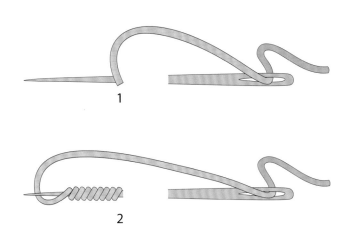

Note To form a Bullion Knot with a slight curve, make more wraps around the tip of the needle than are needed.

French Knot

Bring threaded needle up from wrong to right side of fabric at the position where you want the knot (#1). Wrap the yarn/thread twice around needle. Insert the needle back through the fabric, close to where it came up (almost in the same hole as #1). Gently pull the needle and yarn/thread through the wrapped loops to form the knot.

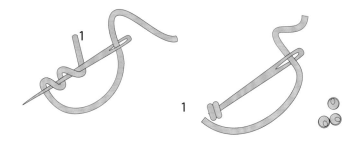

Satin Stitch

Bring threaded needle up from wrong to right side of fabric (#1). Insert needle along desired outline (#2) and bring it out close to #1. Insert it back, close to #2 and out close to previous stitch. Repeat making stitches close to each other following the desired shape. Take care to make even stitches that are not too tight, so that the fabric still lies flat.

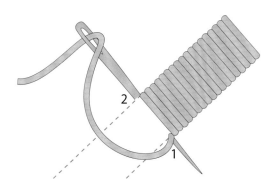

Straight Stitch

Bring threaded needle up from wrong to right side of fabric at the position you want to start the stitch. Insert the needle back into the fabric at the position you want to end the stitch. Repeat for the remaining stitches.

Assembling Amigurumi Pieces Together

Sewing all the amigurumi pieces together can sometimes be a daunting task. Have no fear! There are lots of resources available on the internet showing you how it can be done.

Identifying the Pieces

There are generally three types of pieces that need joining:

1 An "open" piece - where the last round has not been closed. This can be a Body, a Head or even a Limb.

2 A "flat" piece – this is where either where the last round is folded together and crocheted or sewn closed, or it is a single thickness fabric.

3 The other type is what is known as a "closed" piece. This is usually a finished, stuffed piece. Generally, you would attach another piece to this one. Think of a finished, stuffed Body where you need to attach the limbs. You sew through the stitches of the fabric of a closed piece, not through the tops of stitches.

Types of Joining Needed

"Open" to "Open"

This could be where you are joining the last round at the top of the Body to the last round of the neck on the Head. Usually the pieces end up with the same stitch count in the last row and when you join them together you match them, stitch for stitch. One way of sewing this join is using the whipstitch.

"Open" to "Closed"

Examples of this would be joining "open", stuffed limbs to the "closed" Body, or sewing a Muzzle (open) to the face on a Head (closed).

"Flat" to "Closed"

With a Body or Head as the "closed' piece, the Ears, long limbs and Tails could be the "flat" pieces needing attaching.

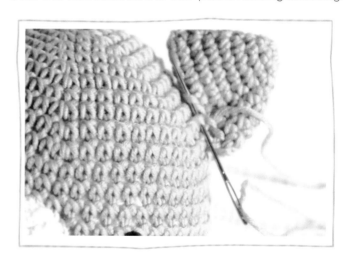

24

Ways of Sewing Joins

There are many different sewing stitches you can use to join pieces together. Everyone develops their own preferences. Practice the various sewing stitch techniques and see which ones you like and which one(s) gives you the nicest finish.

As mentioned, the internet is a great help to identify the "right" sewing stitch for the job and has many tutorials for them. However, the basic stitches used are the Whipstitch and Mattress Stitch (or variation thereof).

Whipstitch

This stitch is commonly used to join "open" to "open" pieces. With both pieces right-side facing, insert your needle through a crocheted stitch on the first piece, from front to back.

Step 1 Bring the needle up through the corresponding stitch on the second piece, from back to front.
Step 2 Insert your needle in the next stitch on the first piece from front to back. Repeat Steps 1 & 2.

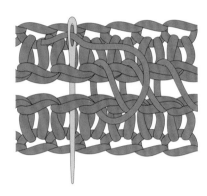

Mattress Stitch

This is a very versatile stitch and can be virtually "invisible" when tugged gently. It can be used for joining most of the types of pieces together.

Both pieces should be right-side facing. Starting on the first piece, insert your needle under a crocheted stitch, from front to back to front.
On the corresponding stitch on the second piece, insert the needle from front to back to front under the stitch.

Step 1 On the first piece, insert your needle in the same place where it came out and bring it up under the next stitch.
Step 2 On the second piece, insert your needle in the same place where it came out and bring it up under the next stitch. Repeat steps 1 & 2.

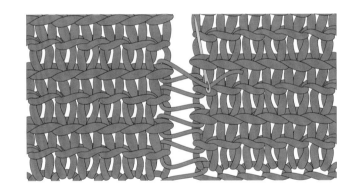

General Tips When Stitching Pieces Together

1 Make sure both pieces you are sewing together are either right-side facing or wrong-side facing (whichever the pattern call for), unless otherwise instructed.

2 When attaching the Head or Limbs to the Body, make sure they are facing the correct way (unless the pattern says differently). For example, the feet on the Legs should usually point to the front of the body.

3 Use straight pins, stuck straight down into a stuffed piece, to position pieces before sewing.

Hint Try placing and pinning the pieces in different positions to give your toy a different 'look'. Once you're happy with the position, you can then sew the pieces together.

4 Where possible, use the same color yarn of at least one of the pieces getting sewn together.

5 When you need to use a separate strand of yarn for sewing the pieces together (not a yarn tail from either piece), start by leaving a long tail for sewing in later. You can tug this tail gently as you go to keep your stitches neat. When you've finished sewing the joins, go back and secure and weave in the front tail.

Hint By doing it this way, it is easier to pull out and fix things if you make a mistake, than trying to unpick a secured starting point.

Backpacking Cat

By Sandrine Deveze

FINISHED SIZE
Cat - about 12" (30.5 cm) tall,
10½" (27 cm) wide – arms open
Backpack - about 4¾" (12 cm) long and
3¼" (8 cm) wide.

MATERIALS NEEDED

For The Cat
DMC Natura Just Cotton
Color A - Moss Green (N75) - for Body
Color B - Ivory (N02) - for Snout and Stomach

For The Backpack
DMC Natura Just Cotton
Color C - Khaki (N20) - for bag base
Color D - Silver Grey (N121) - for bag sides
Color E - Siena (N41) - for claws and button loop
DMC Perle Size 5 Cotton Thread
Color F - Medium Topaz (783) - for handle and pockets

Hook
Size D-3 (3.25 mm) or size suitable for yarn used
Size B-1 (2.25 mm) - for small pockets on Backpack

Other
Polyester Fiberfill for stuffing
¼" (6 mm) Safety Eyes - 2
Colored Embroidery Floss - for Nose (Black) and Mouth (Red)
Cosmetic Blusher for Cheeks
Piece of soft floral fabric: 1¼" (3 cm) wide by 20" (51 cm) long - for Scarf
Square piece of Felt - 4" (10 cm) wide by 5" (13 cm) long - for Bedroll
Button - for Backpack
Yarn Needle, sewing needle, scissors, stitch markers.

CAT

HEAD

ROUND 1: (Right Side) Using Color A and larger hook, make a **Magic Ring** (see Techniques), 6 sc in ring. DO NOT JOIN. (6 sc) Mark last stitch.

ROUND 2: 2 sc in each sc around. (12 sc) Move marker each round.

ROUND 3: [**Inc** (see Special Stitches) in next sc, sc in next sc] around. (18 sc)

ROUND 4: [Inc in next sc, sc in each of next 2 sc] around. (24 sc)

ROUND 5: [Inc in next sc, sc in each of next 3 sc] around. (30 sc)

ROUND 6: [Inc in next sc, sc in each of next 4 sc] around. (36 sc)

ROUND 7: [Inc in next sc, sc in each of next 5 sc] around. (42 sc)

ROUND 8: Sc in each sc around. (42 sc)

ROUND 9: [Inc in next sc, sc in each of next 6 sc] around. (48 sc)

ROUND 10: [Inc in next sc, sc in each of next 7 sc] around. (54 sc)

ROUND 11: [Inc in next sc, sc in each of next 8 sc] around. (60 sc)

ROUNDS 12-18: Sc in each sc around. (60 sc)

ROUND 19: [Inc in next sc, sc in each of next 9 sc] around. (66 sc)

ROUND 20: [**Sc-dec** (see Special Stitches), sc in each of next 9 sc] around. (60 sc)

ROUND 21: [Sc-dec, sc in each of next 8 sc] around. (54 sc)

ROUND 22: [Sc-dec, sc in each of next 7 sc] around. (48 sc)

- Insert Safety Eyes between Rounds 15 & 16, with about 13 stitches between them.

- Start stuffing the Head firmly, adding more as you go.

ROUND 23: [Sc-dec, sc in each of next 6 sc] around. (42 sc)

ROUND 24: [Sc-dec, sc in each of next 5 sc] around. (36 sc)

ROUND 25: [Sc-dec, sc in each of next 4 sc] around. (30 sc)

ROUND 26: [Sc-dec, sc in each of next 3 sc] around. (24 sc)

ROUND 27: [Sc-dec, sc in each of next 2 sc] around. (18 sc) **Fasten off** (see Techniques) leaving long tail for sewing.

- Finish stuffing Head and set aside.

SNOUT

ROUNDS 1-3: Using Color B and larger hook, repeat Rounds 1-3 of Head. At the end of Round 3, there are 18 sc.

ROUNDS 4-17: Sc in each sc around. (18 sc)

At the end of Round 17, fasten off leaving long tail for sewing.

- Fold Snout flat. Do not stuff.

- Using photo as guide, with the Floss and needle, embroider the Nose using **Satin Stitch** and the Mouth using **Straight Stitches** (see Embroidery Stitches).

- Using long tail and yarn needle, sew the opening closed across 9 sts.

Position and sew the Snout between the Eyes on the Head, matching the closed stitches of Snout with stitches on the last round of Head.

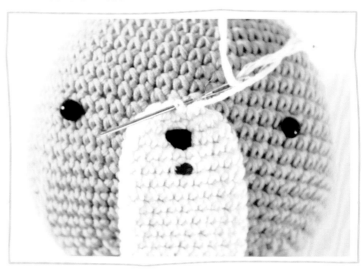

- Apply a little Blusher to the Cheeks.

EARS (Make 2)

ROUND 1: (Right Side) Using Color A and larger hook, make a Magic Ring; 6 sc in ring. DO NOT JOIN. (6 sc) Mark last stitch.

ROUND 2: Sc in each sc around. (6 sc) Move marker each round.

ROUND 3: 2 sc in each sc around. (12 sc)

ROUND 4: Sc in each sc around. (12 sc)

ROUND 5: [Inc in next sc, sc in each of next 2 sc] 4 times. (16 sc) Fasten off leaving long tail for sewing. Do not stuff Ears.

ROUND 6: Sc in each sc around (16 sc)

ROUND 7: [Inc in next sc, sc in each of next 3 sc] 4 times (20 sc)

ROUND 8: Sc in each sc around (20 sc)

- Position and sew Ears on either side of the Head.

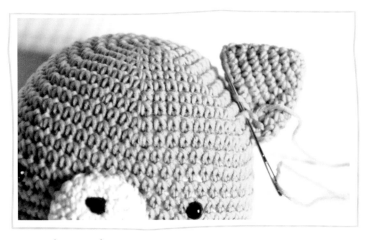

LEGS (Make 2)

ROUND 1: (Right Side) Using Color A and larger hook, make a Magic Ring, 6 sc in ring. DO NOT JOIN. (6 sc) Mark last stitch.

ROUND 2: 2 sc in each sc around. (12 sc) Move marker each round.

ROUND 3: [Inc in next sc, sc in next sc] around. (18 sc)

ROUND 4: [Sc-dec] 3 times, sc in each of next 12 sc. (15 sc)

- Start stuffing Legs firmly, adding more as you go.

ROUNDS 5-30: Sc in each sc around. (15 sc) For the first Leg, at the end of Round 30, fasten off and set aside.

For the second Leg, DO NOT FASTEN OFF. Continue with Body.

BODY

ROUND 1: Holding both Legs together, working in the first Leg, starting from the first st after marker, sc in each of next 15 sc, working in the second Leg, starting at the first st, sc in each of next 15 sc. (30 sc) Mark last stitch.

ROUND 2: Sc in each sc around. (30 sc)

ROUND 3: [Inc in next sc] twice, sc in each of next 7 sc, inc

in next sc, sc in each of next 5 sc, [inc in next sc] twice, sc in each of next 6 sc, inc in next sc, sc in each of next 6 sc. (36 sc),

ROUND 4: Sc in each sc around. (36 sc)

ROUND 5: Sc in each of next 2 sc, inc in next sc, sc in each of next 17 sc, inc in next sc, sc in each of next 15 sc. (38 sc)

ROUND 6: Inc in next sc, sc in each of next 4 sc, inc in next sc, sc in each of next 12 sc, inc in next sc, sc in each of next 5 sc, inc in next sc, sc in each of next 13 sc. (42 sc)

ROUNDS 7-11: Sc in each sc around. (42 sc)

ROUND 12: [Sc-dec, sc in each of next 5 sc] around. (36 sc)

ROUNDS 13-14: Sc in each sc around. (36 sc)

ROUND 15: [Sc-dec, sc in each of next 4 sc] around. (30 sc)

ROUNDS 16-20: Sc in each sc around. (30 sc)

- Start stuffing the Body firmly, adding more as you go.

ROUND 21: [Sc-dec, sc in each of next 3 sc] around. (24 sc)

ROUND 22: Sc in each sc around (24 sc)

ROUND 23: [Sc-dec, sc in each of next 2 sc] around. (18 sc) Fasten off.

- Finish stuffing Body.

- Using long tail from Head and yarn needle, position Head to Body and then matching stitches, sew in place, adding more stuffing to make the neck very firm.

STOMACH

ROUND 1: (Right side) Using Color B and larger hook, ch 10, sc in 2nd ch from hook, sc in each of next 7 ch, 6 sc in last ch; working in unused lps on other side of starting ch, sc in each of next 8 ch, 6 sc in the ch used to turn. DO NOT JOIN. (28 sc) Mark last stitch.

ROUND 2: Sc in each of next 10 sc, inc in next sc, sc in next sc, inc in next sc, sc in each of next 10 sc, inc in next sc, sc in next sc, inc in next sc, sc in each of next 2 sc. (32 sc) Move marker.

ROUND 3: Sc in each of next 10 sc, [inc in next sc, sc in each of next 2 sc] twice, inc in next sc, sc in each of next 10 sc, inc in next sc, sc in each of next 4 sc. (36 sc)

ROUND 4: Sc in each of next 9 sc, [inc in next sc, sc in each of next 2 sc] 4 times, sc in each of next 9 sc, [inc in next sc, sc in each of next 2 sc] twice. (42 sc)

ROUND 5: Sc in each of next 9 sc, [inc in next sc, sc in each of next 3 sc] 4 times, sc in each of next 9 sc, inc in next sc, sc in each of next 5 sc, inc in next sc, sc in next sc. (48 sc)

ROUND 6: Sc in each of next 9 sc, [inc in next sc, sc in each of next 3 sc] 4 times, sc in each of next 2 sc, sl st in next sc. (32 sc) Leave remaining its unworked. Fasten off using Invisible Join (see Techniques) leaving long tail for sewing.

- Using long tail and yarn needle, position and sew Stomach to front of Body (with Round 6 to the bottom near the Legs.)

TAIL

ROUND 1: (Right Side) Using Color A and larger hook, make a Magic Ring, 6 sc in ring. DO NOT JOIN. (6 sc) Mark last stitch.

- Do not stuff Tail

ROUNDS 2 -22: Sc in each sc around. (6 sc)

- At the end of Round 22, fasten off leaving long tail for sewing.

- With photo as guide, Using long tail and yarn needle, sew the tail to center back of body between Round 7 & 8.

ARMS (Make 2)

ROUND 1: (Right Side) Using Color A and larger hook, make a Magic Ring, 6 sc in ring. DO NOT JOIN. (6 sc) Mark last stitch.

ROUND 2: 2 sc in each sc around. (12 sc) Move marker each round.

- Do not stuff Arms.

ROUNDS 3-27: Sc in each sc around. (12 sc)

At the end of Round 27, fasten off leaving long tail for sewing.

- Flatten the tops of Arms and position on either side of Body at Round 21.

- Using long tails and yarn needle, sew Arms in place.

- Using Color E and yarn needle, sew three long stitches to front of each arm and leg for claws.

- Wrap Scarf around Neck.

BACKPACK

Bag

ROUND 1: (Right Side) Using Color C and larger hook, ch 15, 4 sc in 2nd ch from hook, sc in each of next 12 ch, 4 sc in last ch; working in unused lps on other side of starting ch, sc in each of next 12 ch. DO NOT JOIN. (32 sc) Mark last stitch.

ROUND 2: [Inc in each of next 4 sc, sc in each of next 12 sc] twice, **change color** (see Techniques) to Color D in last st. (40 sc) Move marker.

ROUND 3: With color D, working in back loops only sc in each sc around (40 sc)

ROUNDS 4-18: Sc in each sc around. (40 sc)
At the end of Round 18, DO NOT FASTEN OFF. Continue with Bag Flap. Work continues in Rows.

Bag Flap

ROW 1: Sc in each of next 3 sc. Leave rem sts unworked. (16 sc)

ROWS 2-19: Ch 1, turn, sc in each sc across. (14 sc)
At the end of Row 19, fasten off and weave in all ends.

- Sew Button to center front of Bag Flap.

Backpack Straps (make 2)

ROUND 1: (Right Side) Using Color D, starting with a long tail for sewing, make a Magic Ring, 6 sc in ring. DO NOT JOIN. (6 sc) Mark last stitch and move marker each round.

ROUNDS 2-18: Sc in each sc around. (6 sc)
At the end of Round 18, fasten off leaving long tail for sewing.

- With photo as guide, using long tails and yarn needle, sew tops and bottoms of Straps to back of Bag.

Bag Handle

Using Color F and smaller hook, ch 17, sc in 2nd ch from hook, [sc in next ch] across. (16 sc) Fasten off leaving long tail for sewing.

- Using long tail and yarn needle, sew either end of Handle to outside of Bag Flap at around Rows 6-7.

Pockets (Make 2)

ROW 1: (Right Side) Using Color F and smaller hook, ch 14, dc in 4th ch from hook (skipped ch count as first dc), [dc in next ch] across. (12 dc)

ROWS 2-5: Ch 3 (counts as first dc, now and throughout), turn, [dc in next dc] across. (12 dc)
At the end of Row 5, fasten off leaving long tail for sewing.

- Using long tail and yarn needle, position and sew Pockets vertically to front of Bag.

Button Loop

Using Color E and larger hook, ch 28, fasten off leaving long tail for sewing.

- Using long tail and yarn needle, sew both ends of Button Loop center front of Bag, between Pockets, so that it fits around the Button on the Flap.

- Roll up felt Bedroll and place under flap.

Buttons The Bunny

By Mari-Liis Lille

FINISHED SIZE
Larger Bunny - about 11½" (29 cm) tall;
Smaller Bunny - about 7½" (19 cm) tall.

MATERIALS NEEDED

For The Larger Bunny
DMC Natura Medium Just Cotton
Color A - White (#01) - 2 balls - for Head and Arms
Color B - Yellow (#09) - for Body and Legs
Color C - Beige (#31) - for Flower

For The Smaller Bunny
DMC Natura Just Cotton
Color A - Ibiza (N01) - for Head and Arms
Color B - Ble (N83) - for Body and Legs
Color C - Canelle (N37) - for Flower

Hook
For Larger Bunny - Size D-3 (3.25 mm) or size suitable for yarn used.
For Smaller Bunny - Size B-1 (2.25 mm) or size suitable for yarn used.

Other
Pom-pom maker - 1¾" (4.5 cm) for Larger Bunny;
1 ⅜" (3.5 cm) for Smaller Bunny.
Polyester Fiberfill for stuffing
¼" (6 mm) Safety Eyes - 2
Colored Embroidery Floss - for Mouth
Small pieces of Fabric or Felt (optional) - for Cheeks
Yarn Needle, sewing needle, scissors, stitch markers

BUNNY

Note The same pattern is used for both sizes.

HEAD

ROUND 1: (Right Side) Using Color A, make a **Magic Ring** (see Techniques), 6 sc in ring. DO NOT JOIN. (6 sc) Mark last stitch.

ROUND 2: 2 sc in each sc around. (12 sc) Move marker each round.

ROUND 3: [Sc in next sc, **inc** (see Special Stitches) in next sc] around. (18 sc)

ROUND 4: [Sc in each of next 2 sc, inc in next sc] around. (24 sc)

ROUND 5: [Sc in each of next 3 sc, inc in next sc] around. (30 sc)

ROUND 6: [Sc in each of next 4 sc, inc in next sc] around. (36 sc)

ROUND 7: [Sc in each of next 5 sc, inc in next sc] around. (42 sc)

ROUND 8: [Sc in each of next 6 sc, inc in next sc] around. (48 sc)

ROUND 9: [Sc in each of next 7 sc, inc in next sc] around. (54 sc)

ROUNDS 10-19: Sc in each sc around. (54 sc)

- Insert Safety Eyes between Rounds 16 & 17, with about 9-10 stitches between them.

ROUND 20: [Sc in each of next 7 sc, **sc-dec** (see Special Stitches)] around. (48 sc)

ROUND 21: [Sc in each of next 6 sc, sc-dec] around. (42 sc)

ROUND 22: [Sc in each of next 5 sc, sc-dec] around. (36 sc)

ROUND 23: [Sc in each of next 4 sc, sc-dec] around. (30 sc)

- Start stuffing the Head firmly, adding more as you go.

ROUND 24: [Sc in each of next 3 sc, sc-dec] around. (24 sc)

ROUND 25: [Sc in each of next 2 sc, sc-dec] around. (18 sc) **Fasten off** (see Techniques) and weave in ends. Do not close neck opening.

- Finish stuffing Head.

- Using Embroidery Floss, sew small stitches for Mouth using **back stitches** (see Embroidery Stitches).

- Cut small rounds of fabric or felt for Cheeks and sew in place.

EARS (Make 2)

ROUNDS 1-5: Using Color A, rep Rounds 1-5 of Head. At the end of Round 5, there are 30 sc.

ROUNDS 6-11: Sc in each sc around. (30 sc)

ROUND 12: [Sc in each of next 8 sc, sc-dec] 3 times. (27 sc)

ROUND 13: Sc in each sc around. (27 sc)

ROUND 14: [Sc in each of next 7 sc, sc-dec] 3 times. (24 sc)

ROUND 15: Sc in each sc around. (24 sc)

ROUND 16: [Sc in each of next 2 sc, sc-dec] 6 times. (18 sc)

ROUND 17: Sc in each sc around. (18 sc)

ROUND 18: [Sc in each of next 4 sc, sc-dec] 3 times. (15 sc)

ROUND 19: Sc in each sc around. (15 sc)

ROUND 20: [Sc in each of next 3 sc, sc-dec] 3 times. (12 sc)

ROUND 21: Sc in each sc around. (12 sc) Fasten off leaving long tail for sewing. Do not stuff Ears.

- Using photo as guide, position Ears on top of Head.

- Using long tail and yarn needle, sew Ears in place.

FLOWER

ROUND 1: (Right Side) Using Color C, make a Magic Ring; 6 sc in ring. DO NOT JOIN. (6 sc)

ROUND 2: Working in **back loops** only (see Techniques), 2 sc in each sc around. (12 sc) Sl st in back loop of next sc.

ROUND 3: Ch 5, turn, skip sl st, working around spiral (Rnd 2 & Rnd 1) in **back loops** only, [sl st in next sc, ch 5] around, ending with sl st in last sc. (18 petals) Fasten off leaving long tail for sewing.

- Pull long tail through to back of Flower and weave in ends.

- Position Flower on Head, and using a contrasting color of yarn, sew in place through center of Flower.

LEGS (Make 2)

ROUND 1: (Right Side) Using Color B, make a Magic Ring; 6 sc in ring. DO NOT JOIN. (6 sc) Mark last stitch.

ROUND 2: 2 sc in each sc around. (12 sc) Move marker each round.

ROUND 3: [Sc in each of next 3 sc, inc in next sc] 3 times. (15 sc)

ROUNDS 4-10: Sc in each sc around. (15 sc)

For the first Leg, at the end of Round 10, fasten off leaving long tail for sewing, and set aside.

For the second Leg, DO NOT FASTEN OFF. Continue with Joining Round.

JOINING ROUND: Ch 5, working in the first Leg, sc in each of next 15 sc, ch 5, working in second Leg, sc in each sc around. (40 sts) Mark last sc. DO NOT FASTEN OFF. Continue with Body.

BODY

ROUND 1: [Sc in each of next 5 ch, sc in each of next 15 sc] twice. (40 sc) Move marker each round.

ROUNDS 2-11: Sc in each sc around. (40 sc)

- Using long tail from first Leg and yarn needle, sew the opening between the Legs closed.

ROUND 12: [Sc in each of next 6 sc, sc-dec] 5 times. (35 sc)

ROUND 13: Sc in each sc around, **change color** (see Techniques) to Color A in last st. (35 sc)

- Stuff the legs firmly. Start stuffing the Body, adding more as you go.

ROUND 14: With Color A, sc in each sc around. (35 sc)

ROUND 15: [Sc in each of next 5 sc, sc-dec] 5 times. (30 sc)

ROUNDS 16-17: Sc in each sc around. (30 sc)

ROUND 18: [Sc in each of next 3 sc, sc-dec] 6 times. (24 sc)

ROUNDS 19-20: Sc in each sc around. (24 sc)

ROUND 21: [Sc in each of next 2 sc, sc-dec] 6 times. (18 sc) Fasten off leaving long tail for sewing.

- Using long tail and yarn needle, sew the Body to the last round of Head, making sure the face is centered, and adding more stuffing to the Neck, if needed.

- Using Color A, make a pompom Tail and attach it to back of Body.

- Sew a Button to the center Front of Body.

- Using Color B, leaving a long tail for sewing, make a length of chain stitches for the Suspenders, to fit from the upper edge of trousers (at the back), over the shoulder and around the button in front, back over the shoulder to the opposite upper edge of trousers. Fasten off leaving long tail for sewing.

- Using the long tails and yarn needle, sew the chain suspenders in place.

ARMS (Make 2)

ROUND 1: (Right Side) Using Color A, make a Magic Ring; 9 sc in ring. DO NOT JOIN. (9 sc) Mark last stitch.

- After a few rounds, start stuffing Arm firmly, adding as you go. Do not stuff the upper part of the Arms.

ROUNDS 2-14: Sc in each sc around. (9 sc)

ROUND 15: [Sc in next sc, sc-dec] 3 times. (6 sc) Fasten off leaving long tail for sewing.

- Flatten Arm opening, and using long tail and yarn needle, sew across to close opening.

- Position and attach Arms to either side of Body.

Happy Girl

By Kristina Turner

MATERIALS NEEDED

DMC Natura Medium Just Cotton
Color A - Yellow (#09) - for Hair
Color B - Pale Pink (#04) - for Body
Color C - Green (#138) - for Dress

Hook
Size D-3 (3.25 mm) or size suitable for yarn used.

Other
Polyester Fiberfill for stuffing
⅓" (8 mm) Safety Eyes - 2
DMC Cotton Embroidery Floss – Black, for Nose and Mouth
Cosmetic Blusher for cheeks
Yarn Needle, sewing needle, scissors, stitch markers.

Gauge (using Materials above)
23 sc & 23 sc rows = 4" (10 cm) square

DOLL

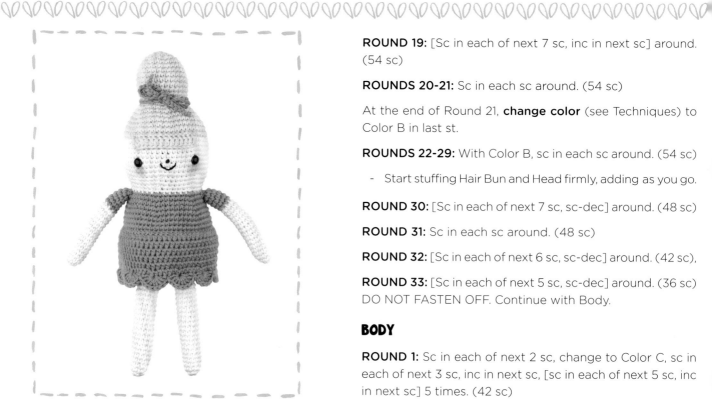

HAIR/HEAD

ROUND 1: (Right Side) Using Color A, make a **Magic Ring** (see Techniques), 6 sc in ring. DO NOT JOIN. (6 sc) Mark last stitch.

ROUND 2: 2 sc in each sc around. (12 sc) Move marker each round.

ROUND 3: [Sc in next sc, **inc** (see Special Stitches) in next sc] around. (18 sc)

ROUND 4: [Sc in each of next 2 sc, inc in next sc] around. (24 sc)

ROUND 5: Sc in each sc around. (24 sc)

ROUND 6: [Sc in each of next 3 sc, inc in next sc] around. (30 sc)

ROUNDS 7-12: Sc in each sc around. (30 sc)

ROUND 13: [Sc in each of next 3 sc, **sc-dec** (see Special Stitches)] around. (24 sc)

ROUND 14: Working in **front loops** only (see Techniques), [sc in each of next 3 sc, inc in next sc] around. (30 sc)

ROUND 15: Working in both loops, [sc in each of next 4 sc, inc in next sc] around. (36 sc)

ROUND 16: [Sc in each of next 5 sc, inc in next sc] around. (42 sc)

ROUND 17: [Sc in each of next 6 sc, inc in next sc] around. (48 sc)

ROUND 18: Sc in each sc around. (48 sc)

ROUND 19: [Sc in each of next 7 sc, inc in next sc] around. (54 sc)

ROUNDS 20-21: Sc in each sc around. (54 sc)

At the end of Round 21, **change color** (see Techniques) to Color B in last st.

ROUNDS 22-29: With Color B, sc in each sc around. (54 sc)

- Start stuffing Hair Bun and Head firmly, adding as you go.

ROUND 30: [Sc in each of next 7 sc, sc-dec] around. (48 sc)

ROUND 31: Sc in each sc around. (48 sc)

ROUND 32: [Sc in each of next 6 sc, sc-dec] around. (42 sc),

ROUND 33: [Sc in each of next 5 sc, sc-dec] around. (36 sc) DO NOT FASTEN OFF. Continue with Body.

BODY

ROUND 1: Sc in each of next 2 sc, change to Color C, sc in each of next 3 sc, inc in next sc, [sc in each of next 5 sc, inc in next sc] 5 times. (42 sc)

ROUND 2: [Sc in each of next 6 sc, inc in next sc] around. (48 sc)

ROUND 3: Sc in each sc around. (48 sc) DO NOT FASTEN OFF.
- Finish stuffing Bun and Head firmly.

- On the front of the Doll's Face (the opposite side of the color change), insert Safety Eyes between Rounds 26 & 27, with 11 sts between them.

Note Instead of Safety Eyes, you can either use Felt circles for the Eyes or embroider them.

Designer's Tips:
- For a larger nose, embroider another French knot over the first one and secure it to the face.

- I went over the mouth twice with floss, to make it thicker and cleaner.

Additional Face Options

Cut Felt Eyes

Embroidered Closed Eyes

- Using 6 strands of floss, embroider a **French knot** for the Nose, and embroider the Mouth using **backstitch** (see Embroidery Stitches).

- Lightly apply pink blusher or eyeshadow to the cheeks (under the eyes), using a make-up brush or a cotton swab.

ROUND 4: [Sc in each of next 7 sc, inc in next sc] around. (54 sc)

ROUND 5: [Sc in each of next 8 sc, inc in next sc] around. (60 sc)

ROUNDS 6-14: Sc in each sc around. (60 sc)

ROUND 15: [Sc in each of next 8 sc, sc-dec] around. (54 sc)

- Start stuffing Body firmly to maintain shape, adding as you go.

ROUND 16: [Sc in each of next 7 sc, sc-dec] around. (48 sc)

ROUND 17: Sc in each sc around. (48 sc)

ROUND 18: [Sc in each of next 6 sc, sc-dec] around. (42 sc)

ROUND 19: [Sc in each of next 5 sc, sc-dec] around. (36 sc)

ROUND 20: [Sc in each of next 4 sc, sc-dec] around. (30 sc)

ROUND 21: [Sc in each of next 3 sc, sc-dec] around. (24 sc)

ROUND 22: [Sc in each of next 2 sc, sc-dec] around. (18 sc)

ROUND 23: [Sc in next sc, sc-dec] around. (12 sc)

ROUND 24: [Sc-dec] around. (6 sc) Fasten off leaving long tail for sewing.

- Finish stuffing the Body.

- Using long tail and yarn needle, close the opening (see Techniques).

HAIR BOW

Using Color C, ch 75. Fasten off.

- Tie a double knot at both ends of the chain, and cut tails close to the knot.

- Wrap chain around Bun and tie a bow in front.

HAIR BANGS

ROW 1: (Right Side) Using Color A, ch 16, dc in 3rd ch from hook (skipped ch count as first dc), [dc in next ch] across. (14 dc) Fasten off leaving long tail for sewing.

Position Bangs on Face, and using the long tail and yarn needle, whipstitch top of Bangs to Round 21 (last round) of Hair and bottom of Bangs to Round 22 (on Face).

LEGS (Make 2)

ROUND 1: (Right Side) Using Color B, make a Magic Ring 6 sc in ring. DO NOT JOIN. (6 sc) Mark last stitch.

ROUND 2: [Sc in next sc, inc in next sc] 3 times. (9 sc) Move marker each round.

ROUND 3: [Sc in each of next 2 sc, inc in next sc] 3 times. (12 sc)

- Start stuffing Legs firmly, adding more as you go.

ROUNDS 4-22: Sc in each sc around. (12 sc)
At the end of Round 22, fasten off leaving long tail for sewing.

- Finish stuffing Leg, stuffing lightly at opening.

Position the Legs towards the front of the Body (not at the sides).

- Using long tails and yarn needle, sew the bottom of Leg opening to stitches on Round 19 and the top of Leg opening to stitches on Round 17. Secure and weave in ends.

ARMS (Make 2)

ROUND 1: (Right Side) Using Color B, make a Magic Ring 7 sc in ring. DO NOT JOIN. (7 sc) Mark last stitch.

ROUND 2: [Sc in next sc, inc in next sc] 3 times, sc in next sc. (10 sc) Move marker each round.

- Start stuffing Arms firmly, adding more as you go.

ROUNDS 3-16: Sc in each sc around. (10 sc)

At the end of Round 16, change to Color C in last st.

ROUNDS 17-21: With Color C, sc in each sc around. (10 sc) At the end of Round 21, fasten off leaving long tail for sewing.

- Finish stuffing Arm, stuffing lightly at opening.

- Using long tails between Rounds 1 & 2. Secure and weave in ends.

Position Arms on either side of Body. Using long tails and yarn needle, sew top of Arm opening to stitches on Round 1.

Sew bottom of Arm opening to stitches on Round 2. Secure and weave in ends.

SKIRT

Note The skirt is worked in joined rounds, not in a spiral.

ROUND 1: (Right Side) Using Color C, leaving about a 20" (51 cm) long tail (to sew Skirt to Body), ch 60; taking care not to twist chain, sl st in first ch to form ring; ch 2 (does NOT count as first hdc, now and throughout), hdc in same st as joining, [hdc in next ch] around; join with sl st to first hdc. (60 hdc)

ROUNDS 2-5: Ch 2, hdc in same st as joining, [hdc in next hdc] around; join with sl st to first hdc. (60 hdc)

ROUND 6: Ch 2, hdc in same st as joining, hdc in each of next 8 hdc, 2 hdc in next hdc, [hdc in each of next 9 hdc, 2 hdc in next hdc] around; join with sl st to first hdc. (66 hdc)

ROUND 7: [Skip next 2 hdc, 7 dc in next hdc, skip next 2 hdc, sl st in next hdc] around. (11 scallops). Fasten off and weave in yarn tail.

- Using long starting tail at Round 9 Secure and weave in ends.

Position Skirt around Body at Round 9. Using long starting tail and yarn needle, with right side facing, sew Skirt in place. Secure and weave in ends.

Cheeky Bird

By Kristina Turner

FINISHED SIZE
About 8½" (22 cm) tall.

MATERIALS NEEDED

DMC Natura Medium Just Cotton
Color A – Mustard Yellow (#99) - for Beak and Legs
Color B – Pale Blue (#07) - for Body
Color C – Pink (#444) - for Shirt

Hook
Size D-3 (3.25 mm) or size suitable for yarn used.

Other
Polyester Fiberfill for stuffing
DMC Cotton Embroidery Floss - Black, for Eyes
(Or Black ¼" (6 mm) Safety Eyes – 2)
Pale Pink Cosmetic Blusher for Cheeks
Yarn Needle, sewing needle, scissors, stitch markers.

Gauge (using Materials above)
23 sc & 23 sc rows = 4" (10 cm) square

BIRD

ADDITIONAL STITCHES USED IN PATTERN

Popcorn (pop): Work 3 double crochets in the same stitch specified, remove hook from loop, insert hook from front to back through the top of first dc made, place loop back on hook and pull dropped loop through stitch. Chain 1 to secure.

Designer's Notes:

1) When working the sc in the next st after popcorn, fold the popcorn stitch towards you to make sure the popcorn stays on the right side.

2) On the next round, work the sc-sts into the ch-stitch under the popcorn.

BEAK

ROUND 1: (Right Side) Using Color A, ch 6, 3 sc in 2nd ch from hook, sc in each of next 3 ch, 3 sc in last ch, working in unused lps on other side of starting ch, sc in each of next 3 ch; join with sl st to first sc. (12 sc) Fasten off leaving long tail for sewing.

Using long end and yarn needle, bring yarn up in center of oval Beak.

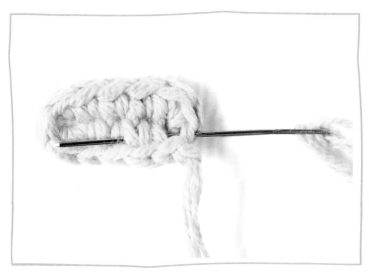

Fold Beak in half and sew the straight sides of oval together. (2 stitches each side.)

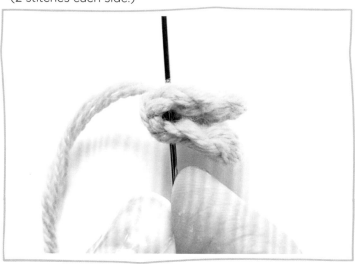

Do not cut yarn. Set finished Beak aside.

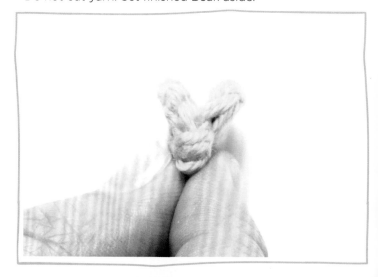

HEAD

ROUND 1: (Right Side) Starting at top of Head, using Color B, leaving a 15" (38 cm) long tail (for head feathers) on right side, make a **Magic Ring** (see Techniques), 6 sc in ring. DO NOT JOIN. (6 sc) Mark last stitch.

ROUND 2: 2 sc in each sc around. (12 sc) Move marker each round.

ROUND 3: [Sc in next sc, **inc** (see Special Stitches) in next sc] around. (18 sc)

ROUND 4: [Sc in each of next 2 sc, inc in next sc] around. (24 sc)

ROUND 5: [Sc in each of next 3 sc, inc in next sc] around. (30 sc)

ROUND 6: Sc in each sc around. (30 sc)

ROUND 7: [Sc in each of next 4 sc, inc in next sc] around. (36 sc)

ROUND 8: [Sc in each of next 5 sc, inc in next sc] around. (42 sc)

ROUND 9: [Sc in each of next 6 sc, inc in next sc] around. (48 sc)

ROUNDS 10-18: Sc in each sc around. (48 sc)

ROUND 19: [Sc in each of next 6 sc, **sc-dec** (see Special Stitches)] around. (42 sc)

ROUND 20: [Sc in each of next 5 sc, sc-dec] around, **change color** (see Techniques) to Color C in last st. (36 sc) DO NOT FASTEN OFF. Continue with Body.

With the color change (marked stitch) as center back of Head, sew the Beak to center front of Head at Round 15, securing the yarn on the inside.

Using Floss and small **back stitches** (see Embroidery Stitches), embroider 'arches' for the Eyes.

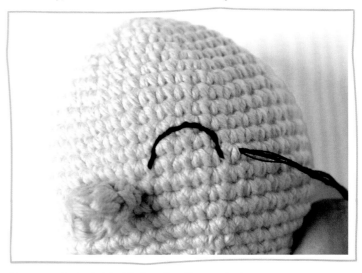

Sew small straight stitches for the eyelashes.

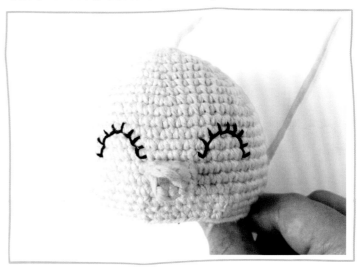

- Lightly apply blusher or eyeshadow to the cheeks, using a make-up brush or a cotton swab.

Additional Face Options

Instead of embroidering the eyes, use round safety eyes.

Option using Safety Eyes

Using starting tail and yarn needle, make Head Feathers inserting yarn into top of head, leaving a loop on the outside.

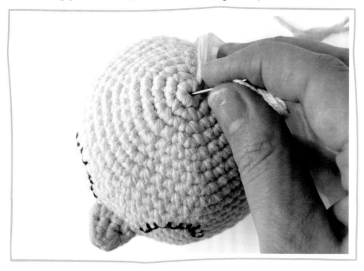

Make a double knot on the inside to secure loop.

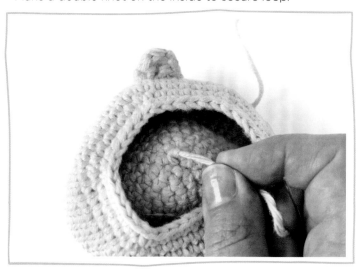

Bring yarn needle back out through top of Head and make 2 more loops – 3 loops in total.

- Stuff Head firmly.

BODY

ROUND 1: With Color C, [sc in each of next 5 sc, inc in next sc] around. (42 sc)

ROUND 2: [Sc in each of next 6 sc, inc in next sc] around. (48 sc)

ROUND 3: [Sc in each of next 7 sc, inc in next sc] around. (54 sc)

ROUND 4: [Sc in each of next 4 sc, **pop** (see Additional Stitches) in next sc, sc in each of next 3 sc, inc in next sc] around. (60 sts)

ROUNDS 5-6: Sc in each sc around. (60 sc)

ROUND 7: [Sc in each of next 9 sc, pop in next sc] around. (60 sts)

ROUNDS 8-9: Sc in each sc around. (60 sc)

ROUND 10: Sc in each of next 4 sc, pop in next sc, [sc in each of next 9 sc, pop in next sc] 5 times, sc in each of next 5 sc. (60 sts)

ROUND 11: Sc in each sc around, change to Color B in last st. (60 sc)

ROUND 12: With Color B, sc in each sc around. (60 sc)

ROUND 13: [Sc in each of next 8 sc, sc-dec] around. (54 sc)

ROUND 14: [Sc in each of next 7 sc, sc-dec] around. (48 sc)

ROUND 15: [Sc in each of next 6 sc, sc-dec] around. (42 sc)

ROUND 16: Sc in each sc around. (42 sc)

ROUND 17: [Sc in each of next 5 sc, sc-dec] around. (36 sc)

ROUND 18: [Sc in each of next 4 sc, sc-dec] around. (30 sc)

- Start stuffing Body firmly to maintain shape, adding more as you go.

ROUND 19: [Sc in each of next 3 sc, sc-dec] around. (24 sc)

ROUND 20: [Sc in each of next 2 sc, sc-dec] around. (18 sc)

ROUND 21: [Sc in next sc, sc-dec] around. (12 sc)

ROUND 22: [Sc-dec] around. (6 sc) Fasten off leaving long tail for sewing.

- Finish stuffing the Body.

- Using long tail and yarn needle, **close the opening** (see Techniques).

WINGS (make 2)

ROW 1: (Right Side) Using Color B, leaving a 15" (38 cm) long tail for sewing to Body, ch 7, sc in 2nd ch from hook, [sc in next ch] across. (6 sc)

ROW 2: Ch 1, turn, 2 sc in first sc, sc in each of next 4 sc, 2 sc in last sc. (8 sc)

ROWS 3-5: Ch 1, turn, sc in each sc across. (8 sc)

ROW 6: Ch 1, turn, using first 2 sts, **sc2tog** (see Special Stitches), sc in each of next 4 sc, sc2tog using last 2 sts. (6 sc)

ROW 7: Ch 1, turn, sc in each sc across. (6 sc)

ROW 8: Ch 1, turn, using first 2 sts, sc2tog, sc in each of next 2 sc, sc2tog using last 2 sts. (4 sc)

ROW 9: Ch 1, turn, sc in each sc across. (4 sc)

ROW 10: Ch 1, turn, using first 2 sts, sc2tog, sc2tog using last 2 sts. (2 sc)

ROW 11: Ch 1, turn, sc in each sc across. (2 sc)

ROW 12: Ch 1, turn, using both sts, sc2tog. (1 sc) Fasten off and weave in end tail.

- Using starting tail and yarn needle, position and sew first row of each Wing to either side of Round 2 of Body.

LEGS (Make 2)

ROUND 1: (Right Side) Using Color A, make a Magic Ring, 6 sc in ring. DO NOT JOIN. (6 sc) Mark last stitch.

- Do not stuff Legs.

ROUNDS 2-15: Sc in each sc around. (6 sc)
At the end of Round 15, fasten off leaving long tail for sewing.

FEET (Make 2)

ROUND 1: (Right Side) Using Color A, leave a 10" (25.5 cm) long tail on right side, make a Magic Ring, 7 sc in ring. DO NOT JOIN. (7 sc)

ROUND 2: Sl st in next sc, [ch 3, sc in 2nd ch from hook, hdc in next ch, working in Round 1, sl st in next sc] 3 times. Leave rem sts unworked. (3 Toes) Fasten off and weave in end tail.

- Using starting long tail and yarn needle, sew center of each Foot to center of Leg Round 1.

Position Legs between Rounds 16 & 17 towards front of Body.

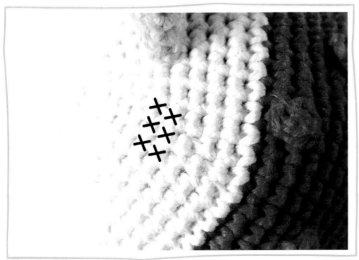

Flatten tops of Legs, with Feet facing forward, and using long tail, whipstitch in position.

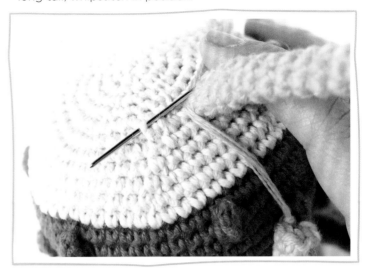

Repeat for other Leg.

Heart Cat

By Kristina Turner

FINISHED SIZE
About 11½" (29 cm) tall.

MATERIALS NEEDED

DMC Natura Medium Just Cotton
Color A – Yellow (#09) - for Body
Color B – Mint (#137) - for Pajamas
Color C – Pink (#444) - for Heart

Hook
Size C-2 (2.75 mm) or size suitable for yarn used.

Other
Polyester Fiberfill for stuffing
⅞" (22mm) Cat Safety Eyes - 2 (optional – you can use
regular safety eyes or embroider eyes)
DMC Cotton Embroidery Floss - Black, for Nose and Mouth
Yarn Needle, sewing needle, scissors, stitch markers.

Gauge (using Materials above)
23 sc & 23 sc rows = 4" (10 cm) square

CAT

EARS (Make 2)

ROUND 1: (Right Side) Using Color A, make a **Magic Ring** (see Techniques), 4 sc in ring. DO NOT JOIN. (4 sc) Mark last stitch.

ROUND 2: [Sc in next sc, **inc** (see Special Stitches) in next sc] twice. (6 sc) Move marker each round.

ROUND 3: [Sc in each of next 2 sc, inc in next sc] twice. (8 sc)

ROUND 4: [Sc in each of next 3 sc, inc in next sc] twice. (10 sc)

ROUND 5: [Sc in each of next 4 sc, inc in next sc] twice. (12 sc)

ROUND 6: [Sc in each of next 5 sc, inc in next sc] twice. (14 sc) Leave stitch marker in last st.

At the end of the first Ear, fasten off and weave in all ends. (Use yarn tails to stuff Ears) At the end of the second Ear, DO NOT FASTEN OFF. Secure magic ring and weave in starting tail.

Joining Round: Starting with second Ear, ch 10, taking care not to twist chain and having both Ear tips pointing down, sl st in marked st on first Ear, working in first Ear, sc in next sc, move marker to stitch just made (new first st of rounds), sc in each of next 12 sc, sc in same sc as sl st (14 sc), working in **back ridge** of ch-sts (see Techniques), sc in each of next 10 ch, working in second Ear, sc in each of

next 14 sc (remove marker), working in ch-sts, sc in each of next 10 ch. (48 sc) (The next stitch is the marked first stitch of the round.) DO NOT FASTEN OFF. Continue with Head.

HEAD

ROUND 1: Sc in each sc around. (48 sc)

ROUND 2: Sc in each of next 3 sc, inc in next sc, [sc in each of next 7 sc, inc in next sc] 5 times, sc in each of next 4 sc. (54 sc)

ROUNDS 3-14: Sc in each sc around. (54 sc)

ROUND 15: Sc in each of next 5 sc, **sc-dec** (see Special Stitches), [sc in each of next 7 sc, sc-dec] 5 times, sc in each of next 2 sc. (48 sc)

ROUND 16: Sc in each of next 4 sc, sc-dec, [sc in each of next 6 sc, sc-dec] 5 times, sc in each of next 2 sc. (42 sc)

ROUND 17: Sc in each of next 4 sc, inc in next sc, [sc in each of next 6 sc, inc in next sc] 5 times, **change color** (see Techniques) to Color B in last sc worked, using Color B, sc in each of next 2 sc. (48 sc) DO NOT FASTEN OFF. Continue with Body.

BODY

ROUND 1: Sc in each of next 2 sc, inc in next sc, [sc in each of next 5 sc, inc in next sc] 7 times, sc in each of next 3 sc. (56 sc)

ROUND 2: Sc in each of next 3 sc, inc in next sc, [sc in each of next 6 sc, inc in next sc] 7 times, sc in each of next 3 sc. (64 sc) DO NOT FASTEN OFF.

- On the front of the Cat's Face (the opposite side of the stitch marker and color change), insert Safety Eyes between Rounds 8 & 9, with 11 sts between them.

Note Instead of Safety Eyes, you can also embroider the Eyes.

Designer's Tip: I went over the mouth twice with floss, to make it thicker and cleaner.

Additional Face Options

Open Eyes

Sleepy Eyes

- Using 6 strands of floss, embroider the Nose using **backstitch** and **satin stitches** (see Embroidery Stitches), and the Mouth using backstitch.

ROUND 3: Following the Color Chart for the Heart, sc in each of next 24 sc, change to Color C, with Color C (carrying Color B), sc in each of next 4 sc, change to Color B, with Color B (carrying Color C), sc in each of next 5 sc, change to Color C, with Color C (carrying Color B), sc in each of next 4 sc, change to Color B, with Color B, [sc in next sc] around. (64 sc) Cut Color C.

Notes for Color Chart:

a) Each block represents 1 single crochet stitch.

b) The chart is worked from the bottom-up and from right to left.

c) Carry Color B (by working over the yarn) when working Color C.

d) Carry Color C (by working over the yarn) when working Color B in Rounds 3 to 5.

e) Cut Color C at the end of each round, leaving long tails.

Hint Place stitch markers on the 23rd and 39th stitch.

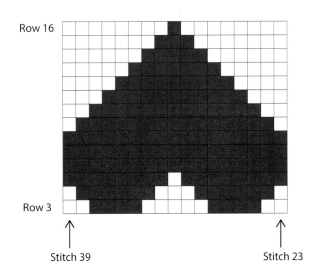

Row 16

Row 3

Stitch 39   Stitch 23

ROUNDS 4-16: Following the Color Chart, sc in each sc around, changing color in the indicated stitches. (64 sc)

ROUNDS 17-19: Using Color B, sc in each sc around. (64 sc)

Tie the loose tails of Color C together in pairs, with the knots on the inside of the Body. Trim the tails.

ROUND 20: [Sc in each of next 6 sc, sc-dec] 8 times. (56 sc)

ROUND 21: [Sc in each of next 5 sc, sc-dec] 8 times. (48 sc)

ROUND 22: [Sc in each of next 4 sc, sc-dec] 8 times. (40 sc)

- Start stuffing the Body firmly to maintain shape, adding more as you go.

ROUND 23: [Sc in each of next 3 sc, sc-dec] 8 times. (32 sc)

ROUND 24: [Sc in each of next 2 sc, sc-dec] 8 times. (24 sc)

ROUND 25: [Sc in next sc, sc-dec] 8 times. (16 sc)

ROUND 26: [Sc-dec] 8 times. (8 sc) Fasten off leaving long tail for sewing.

- Finish stuffing the Body.

- Using long tail and yarn needle, **close the opening** (see Techniques).

LEGS (Make 2)

ROUND 1: (Right Side) Using Color A, make a Magic Ring 6 sc in ring. DO NOT JOIN. (6 sc) Mark last stitch.

ROUND 2: [Sc in next sc, inc in next sc] 3 times. (9 sc) Move marker each round.

ROUND 3: [Sc in each of next 2 sc, inc in next sc] 3 times. (12 sc)

ROUNDS 4-5: Sc in each sc around. (12 sc)
At the end of Round 5, change to Color B in last st.

- Start stuffing Legs firmly, adding more as you go.

ROUNDS 6-23: With Color B, sc in each sc around. (12 sc) At the end of Round 23, fasten off leaving long tail for sewing.

- Finish stuffing Leg, stuffing lightly at opening.

Position the Legs towards the front of the Body (not at the sides).

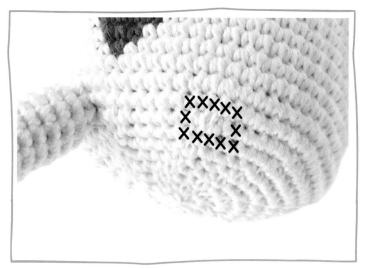

Using long tails and yarn needle, sew the bottom of Leg opening to stitches on Round 20.

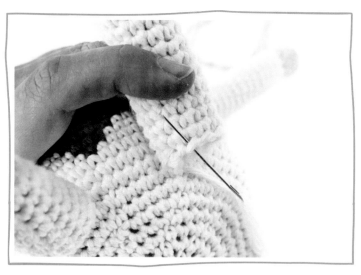

Sew the top of Leg opening to stitches on Round 18. Secure and weave in ends.

ARMS (Make 2)

ROUND 1: (Right Side) Using Color A, make a Magic Ring, 5 sc in ring. DO NOT JOIN. (5 sc) Mark last stitch.

ROUND 2: [Inc in next sc] 5 times. (10 sc) Move marker each round.

ROUNDS 3-5: Sc in each sc around. (10 sc)

At the end of Round 5, change to Color B in last st.

- Start stuffing Arms firmly, adding more as you go.

ROUNDS 6-22: With Color B, sc in each sc around. (10 sc) At the end of Round 22, fasten off leaving long tail for sewing.

- Finish stuffing Arm, stuffing lightly at opening.

Position Arms on either side of the Body. Using long tails and yarn needle, sew top of Arm opening to stitches on Round 2.

Sew bottom of Arm opening to stitches on Round 3. Secure and weave in ends.

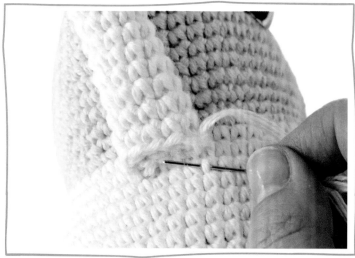

TAIL

ROUND 1: (Right Side) Using Color A, make a Magic Ring 6 sc in ring. DO NOT JOIN. (6 sc) Mark last stitch.

ROUND 2: Sc in each of next 2 sc, inc in next sc] twice. (8 sc) Move marker each round.

ROUND 3: [Sc in each of next 3 sc, inc in next sc] twice. (10 sc)

ROUND 4: [Sc in each of next 4 sc, inc in next sc] twice. (12 sc)

- Start stuffing the Tail firmly, adding as you go.

ROUNDS 5-18: Sc in each of sc around. (12 sc)

ROUNDS 19-23: Sc in each of next 6 sc, hdc in each of next 6 sc. (12 sts)

At the end of Round 23, fasten off leaving long tail for sewing.

- Finish stuffing the Tail firmly.

- Using long tail and yarn needle, whipstitch the opening closed.

- With the hdc-sts on the Tail facing outwards, sew the last round of the Tail to center back of Body at Round 18.

- Then sew across the second-to-last round of the Tail to Round 17 of Body. (This makes the Tail stand up.) Secure and weave in ends.

Lily The Elephant

By Dilek Yıldırım

FINISHED SIZE
About 6½" (16,5 cm) tall;
8" (20 cm) wide – with open ears.

MATERIALS NEEDED

DMC Natura Just Cotton
Color A - Salomé (N80)
Color B - Rose de Meaux (N94) - for Body and Flower
Color C - Aguamarine (N25) - for Flower
Color D - Ivory (N02) - for Inner Ear

Hook
Size B-1 (2.25 mm) or size suitable for yarn used.

Other
Polyester Fiberfill for stuffing
½" (12mm) Safety Eyes - 2
Tulle Fabric - 6" x 20" (15 x 51 cm) - for Skirt
Cosmetic Blusher
Yarn Needle, sewing needle, scissors, stitch markers.

ELEPHANT

HEAD

ROUND 1: (Right Side) Using Color A, make a **Magic Ring** (see Techniques), 6 sc in ring. DO NOT JOIN. (6 sc) Mark last stitch.

ROUND 2: 2 sc in each sc around. (12 sc) Move marker each round.

ROUND 3: [Sc in next sc, **inc** (see Special Stitches) in next sc] around. (18 sc)

ROUND 4: [Sc in each of next 2 sc, inc in next sc] around. (24 sc)

ROUND 5: [Sc in each of next 3 sc, inc in next sc] around. (30 sc)

ROUND 6: [Sc in each of next 4 sc, inc in next sc] around. (36 sc)

ROUND 7: [Sc in each of next 5 sc, inc in next sc] around. (42 sc)

ROUND 8: [Sc in each of next 6 sc, inc in next sc] around. (48 sc)

ROUND 9: [Sc in each of next 7 sc, inc in next sc] around. (54 sc)

ROUND 10: [Sc in each of next 8 sc, inc in next sc] around. (60 sc)

ROUND 11: [Sc in each of next 9 sc, inc in next sc] around. (66 sc)

ROUNDS 12-21: Sc in each sc around. (66 sc)

- Insert Safety Eyes between Rounds 18 & 19, with about 14 stitches between them.

- Start stuffing the Head, adding more as you go.

ROUND 22: [Sc in each of next 9 sc, **sc-dec** (see Special Stitches)] 6 times. (60 sc)

ROUND 23: [Sc in each of next 8 sc, sc-dec] 6 times. (54 sc)

ROUND 24: [Sc in each of next 7 sc, sc-dec] 6 times. (48 sc)

ROUND 25: [Sc in each of next 6 sc, sc-dec] 6 times. (42 sc)

ROUND 26: [Sc in each of next 5 sc, sc-dec] 6 times. (36 sc)

ROUND 27: [Sc in each of next 4 sc, sc-dec] 6 times. (30 sc)

ROUND 28: [Sc in each of next 3 sc, sc-dec] 6 times. (24 sc)

ROUND 29: [Sc in each of next 2 sc, sc-dec] 6 times. (18 sc)

ROUND 30: Sc in each sc around, **changing color** (see Techniques) to Color B in last st. (18 sc) Cut Color A and weave in ends. DO NOT FASTEN OFF COLOR B. Do not close opening.

- Finish stuffing the Head.

INNER EARS (make 2)

ROUND 1: (Right Side) Using Color D, make a Magic Ring, 6 sc in ring. DO NOT JOIN. (6 sc) Mark last stitch.

ROUND 2: 2 sc in each sc around. (12 sc) Move marker each round.

ROUND 3: [Sc in next sc, inc in next sc] around. (18 sc)

ROUND 4: [Sc in each of next 2 sc, inc in next sc] around. (24 sc)

ROUND 5: [Sc in each of next 3 sc, inc in next sc] around. (30 sc)

ROUND 6: [Sc in each of next 4 sc, inc in next sc] around. (36 sc)

ROUND 7: [Sc in each of next 5 sc, inc in next sc] around. (42 sc)

ROUNDS 8-9: Sc in each sc around. (42 sc)
At the end of Round 9, **fasten off** (see Techniques) and weave in ends.

OUTER EARS (make 2)

ROUNDS 1-9: Using Color A, repeat Rounds 1-9 of Inner Ears. DO NOT FASTEN OFF.

ROUND 10: Holding an Outer Ear and Inner Ear, with right sides facing (wrong sides together), working through both thicknesses and matching stitches, sc in each sc around. Fasten off leaving long tail for sewing. (Do not stuff the Ears.)

- Shape Ears and position on Head.

- Using long tail and yarn needle, sew Ears in place.

TRUNK

ROUND 1: (Right Side) Using Color A, make a Magic Ring, 6 sc in ring. DO NOT JOIN. (6 sc) Mark last stitch.

ROUND 2: 2 sc in each sc around. (12 sc) Move marker each round.

ROUNDS 3-12: Sc in each sc around. (12 sc)

ROUND 13: [Sc in each of next 5 sc, inc in next sc] twice. (14 sc)

ROUNDS 14-15: Sc in each sc around. (14 sc)

ROUND 16: [Sc in each of next 6 sc, inc in next sc] twice. (16 sc)

ROUND 17: Sc in each sc around. (16 sc) Fasten off leaving long tail for sewing.

- Lightly stuff the Trunk.

- Position the Trunk between the Eyes on the Head.

- Using long tail and yarn needle, sew Trunk in place.

FLOWER

Flower Center

ROUND 1: (Right Side) Using Color C, starting with long tail, make a Magic Ring, ch 2 (does NOT count as first hdc, now and throughout), 6 hdc in ring; join with sl st to first hdc. (6 hdc)

ROUND 2: Ch 2, working in **front loops** only (see Techniques), hdc in each hdc around; join with sl st to first hdc. (6 hdc) Fasten off using **Invisible Join** (see Techniques) and weave in all ends.

Petals

ROUND 1: With right side of Flower Center facing, working behind Round 2, using Color B, **join with sc** (see Techniques) to **back loop** of any hdc in Round 1, working in **back loops** only (see Techniques), [ch 1, sc in next hdc on Round 1] around, ch 1; join with sl st to first sc. (6 sc & 6 ch-1 sps)

ROUND 2: Ch 1, sc in same st as joining, *ch 3, 3 dc in next ch-1 sp, ch 3**, sc in next sc; repeat from * around, ending at ** on final repeat; join with sl st to first sc. (6 sc & 6 petals)

Fasten off and weave in all ends.

- Using starting long tail of Flower Center and yarn needle, position and sew Flower to top of Head.

- Apply a little Blusher to the Cheeks.

BODY

ROUND 1: Continuing from Head, using Color B, [sc in each of next 2 sc, inc in next sc] around. (24 sc)

ROUND 2: [Sc in each of next 3 sc, inc in next sc] around. (30 sc)

ROUND 3: [Sc in each of next 4 sc, inc in next sc] around. (36 sc)

ROUND 4: [Sc in each of next 5 sc, inc in next sc] around. (42 sc)

ROUNDS 5-11: Sc in each sc around. (42 sc)
At the end of Round 11, change color to Color A in last st.

ROUND 12: With Color A, [sc in each of next 6 sc, inc in next sc] around. (48 sc)

ROUND 13: Sc in each sc around. (48 sc)

- Start stuffing the Body, adding more as you go. (Make sure Neck is firmly stuffed to support Head.)

ROUND 14: [Sc in each of next 6 sc, sc-dec] 6 times. (42 sc)

ROUND 15: [Sc in each of next 5 sc, sc-dec] 6 times. (36 sc)

ROUND 16: [Sc in each of next 4 sc, sc-dec] 6 times. (30 sc)

ROUND 17: [Sc in each of next 3 sc, sc-dec] 6 times. (24 sc)

ROUND 18: [Sc in each of next 2 sc, sc-dec] 6 times. (18 sc)

ROUND 19: [Sc in next sc, sc-dec] 6 times. (12 sc)

ROUND 20: [sc-dec] 6 times. (6 sc) Fasten off leaving long tail.

- Finish stuffing Body.

- Using yarn needle and long tail, **close the opening** (see Techniques).

TUTU SKIRT

Cut the Tulle into strips about ⅜" (1 cm) wide and about 4" (10 cm) long (42 strips are needed).

Working around Round 9 of Body, for each stitch:

- Fold a strip in half.

- Insert hook around post of any sc on Round 9 of Body and place the folded end on hook.

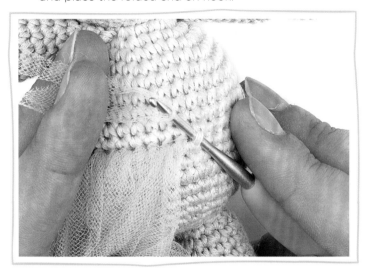

- Pull the Tulle strip half-way through stitch, and then bring the 2 ends through the folded piece, tugging gently to secure.

- Continue around all 42 stitches of Round 9.

ARMS (make 2)

ROUND 1: (Right Side) Using Color A, make a Magic Ring, 6 sc in ring. DO NOT JOIN. (6 sc) Mark last stitch.

ROUND 2: 2 sc in each sc around. (12 sc) Move marker each round.

ROUNDS 3-17: Sc in each sc around. (12 sc)

ROUND 18: [Sc in each of next 2 sc, sc-dec] 3 times. (9 sc) Fasten off leaving long tail for sewing.

- Lightly stuff the Arms.

- Position the Arms on either side of the Body.

- Using long tail and yarn needle, sew Arms in place.

LEGS (make 2)

ROUND 1: (Right Side) Using Color A, make a Magic Ring, 6 sc in ring. DO NOT JOIN. (6 sc) Mark last stitch.

ROUND 2: 2 sc in each sc around. (12 sc) Move marker each round.

ROUND 3: [Sc in next sc, inc in next sc] around. (18 sc)

ROUND 4: [Sc in each of next 2 sc, inc in next sc] around. (24 sc)

ROUND 5: Working in back loops only, sc in each sc around. (24 sc)

ROUNDS 6-7: Working through both loops, sc in each sc around. (24 sc)

ROUND 8: Sc in each of next 8 sc, [sc-dec] 4 times, sc in each of next 8 sc. (20 sc)

ROUND 9: Sc in each of next 7 sc, [sc-dec] 3 times, sc in each of next 7 sc. (17 sc)

ROUND 10: Sc in each of next 6 sc, [sc-dec] twice, sc in each of next 7 sc. (15 sc)

ROUNDS 11-18: Sc in each sc around. (15 sc)

ROUND 19: [Sc in each of next 3 sc, sc-dec] 3 times. (12 sc) Fasten off leaving long tail for sewing.

- Stuff the Legs firmly.

- Position the Legs at the bottom of the Body.

- Using long tail and yarn needle, sew Legs in place.

Leo The Lion

By Dilek Yıldırım

FINISHED SIZE
About 7" (18 cm) tall - sitting,
8" (20 cm) wide - legs open.

MATERIALS NEEDED

DMC Natura Just Cotton
Color A - Tournesol (N16) for the Body
Color B - Brique (N86) for Paws
Mouth Color - Noir (N11)

DMC Woolly
Color C - Orange (102)

Hook
Size B-1 (2.25 mm) or size suitable for yarn used.

Other
Polyester Fiberfill for stuffing
½" (12mm) Safety Eyes - 2
0.55" (14mm) Safety Nose - 1
Cosmetic Blusher
Yarn Needle, sewing needle, scissors, stitch markers.

LION

Bring the hook up and around the front strand of the loop, catching the back strand of the loop and drawing it through the stitch (2 loops on hook). Yarn over and draw through both loops on hook (sc made). Remove finger.

ADDITIONAL STITCHES USED IN PATTERN

Loop Stitch (for Mane and Tail): With the yarn draped over the index finger of the non-hook hand, to form a loop, insert hook around post of next sc.

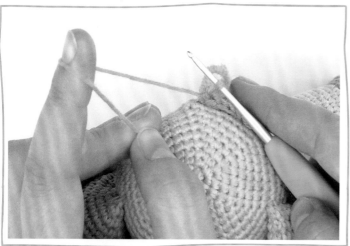

HEAD

ROUND 1: (Right Side) Using Color A, make a **Magic Ring** (see Techniques), 6 sc in ring. DO NOT JOIN. (6 sc) Mark last stitch.

ROUND 2: 2 sc in each sc around. (12 sc) Move marker each round.

ROUND 3: [Sc in next sc, **inc** (see Special Stitches) in next sc] around. (18 sc)

ROUND 4: [Sc in each of next 2 sc, inc in next sc] around. (24 sc)

ROUND 5: [Sc in each of next 3 sc, inc in next sc] around. (30 sc)

ROUND 6: [Sc in each of next 4 sc, inc in next sc] around. (36 sc)

ROUND 7: [Sc in each of next 5 sc, inc in next sc] around. (42 sc)

ROUND 8: [Sc in each of next 6 sc, inc in next sc] around. (48 sc)

ROUND 9: [Sc in each of next 7 sc, inc in next sc] around. (54 sc)

ROUND 10: [Sc in each of next 8 sc, inc in next sc] around. (60 sc)

ROUNDS 11-24: Sc in each sc around. (60 sc)

- Insert Safety Eyes between Rounds 14 & 15, with about 8 stitches between them.

- Insert the Safety Nose between the Eyes on Round 17.

- Stuff the Head as you go.

ROUND 25: [Sc in each of next 8 sc, **sc-dec** (see Special Stitches)] 6 times. (54 sc)

ROUND 26: [Sc in each of next 7 sc, sc-dec] 6 times. (48 sc)

ROUND 27: [Sc in each of next 6 sc, sc-dec] 6 times. (42 sc)

ROUND 28: [Sc in each of next 5 sc, sc-dec] 6 times. (36 sc)

ROUND 29: [Sc in each of next 4 sc, sc-dec] 6 times. (30 sc)

ROUND 30: [Sc in each of next 3 sc, sc-dec] 6 times. (24 sc)
Fasten off (see Techniques) leaving a long tail for sewing.

- Stuff Head firmly.

- Using yarn needle and long tail, **close the opening** (see Techniques).

- Using photo as guide, with Mouth Color and yarn needle, embroider a mouth and freckles, using **back stitches** and **straight stitches** (see Embroidery stitches).

EARS (Make 2)

ROUND 1: (Right Side) Using Color A, make a Magic Ring, 6 sc in ring. DO NOT JOIN. (6 sc) Mark last stitch.

ROUND 2: [Sc in next sc, inc in next sc] 3 times. (9 sc) Move marker each round.

ROUND 3: [Sc in each of next 2 sc, inc in next sc] around. (12 sc)

ROUND 4: [Sc in each of next 3 sc, inc in next sc] around. (15 sc)

ROUND 5: [Sc in each of next 4 sc, inc in next sc] around. (18 sc)

ROUND 6: [Sc in each of next 5 sc, inc in next sc] around. (21 sc)

ROUND 7: [Sc in each of next 6 sc, inc in next sc] around. (24 sc)

ROUNDS 8-9: Sc in each sc around. (24 sc)

At the end of Round 9, fasten off leaving a long tail for sewing. (Do not stuff the Ears.)

- Using yarn needle and long tail, fold each Ear and sew to secure.

- Position and sew Ears to Head.

BODY

ROUNDS 1-10: Using Color A, repeat rounds 1-10 of Head. At the end of Round 10, there are 60 sc.

ROUND 11: [Sc in each of next 8 sc, sc-dec] 6 times. (54 sc)

ROUNDS 12-17: Sc in each sc around. (54 sc)

ROUND 18: [Sc in each of next 7 sc, sc-dec] 6 times. (48 sc)

ROUNDS 19-20: Sc in each sc around. (48 sc)

ROUND 21: [Sc in each of next 6 sc, sc-dec] 6 times. (42 sc)

ROUND 22: Sc in each sc around. (42 sc)
- Start stuffing Body firmly, adding more as you go.

ROUND 23: [Sc in each of next 5 sc, sc-dec] 6 times. (36 sc)

ROUND 24: Sc in each sc around. (36 sc)

ROUND 25: [Sc in each of next 4 sc, sc-dec] 6 times. (30 sc)

ROUNDS 26-27: Sc in each sc around. (30 sc)

ROUND 28: [Sc in each of next 3 sc, sc-dec] 6 times. (24 sc)

ROUNDS 29-32: Sc in each sc around. (24 sc)

At the end of Round 32, fasten off leaving a long tail for sewing.

- Using long tail and yarn needle, sew the Body to the second last round of Head, stuffing firmly before finishing.

ARMS (Make 2)

ROUND 1: (Right Side) Using Color B, make a Magic Ring, 6 sc in ring. DO NOT JOIN. (6 sc) Mark last stitch.

ROUND 2: 2 sc in each sc around. (12 sc) Move marker each round.

ROUND 3: [Sc in next sc, inc in next sc] around. (18 sc)

ROUND 4: [Sc in each of next 2 sc, inc in next sc] around. (24 sc)

ROUND 5: [Sc in each of next 3 sc, inc in next sc] around. (30 sc)

ROUND 6: Working in **back loops** only (see Techniques), sc in each sc around. (30 sc)

ROUNDS 7-8: Working through both loops, sc in each sc around. (30 sc)

ROUND 9: [Sc in each of next 3 sc, sc-dec] 4 times, sc in each of next 10 sc. (26 sc)

ROUND 10: [Sc in each of next 2 sc, sc-dec] 4 times, sc in each of next 10 sc. (22 sc)

ROUND 11: [Sc in next sc, sc-dec] 4 times, sc in each of next 10 sc, **change color** (see Techniques) to Color A in last st. (18 sc) Cut Color B, leaving a long tail for making paws.

- Start stuffing Arms, adding more as you go.

ROUNDS 12-29: Using Color A, sc in each sc around. (18 sc)

ROUND 30: [Sc in next sc, sc-dec] 6 times. (12 sc) Fasten off Color A, leaving long tail for sewing.

- Finish stuffing the Arms lightly.

- Using Color A long tail and yarn needle, flatten last round and sew across 6 sts to close.

- Position Arms on either side of Body at about Round 26 and sew in place.

- Using Color B long tails and yarn needle, insert needle up through magic ring up to last round of Color B. Pull gently to shape and repeat twice more to create paws.

LEGS (Make 2)

ROUNDS 1-5: Using Color B, repeat rounds 1-5 of Lion Arms. At the end of Round 5, there are 30 sc.

ROUND 6: [Sc in each of next 4 sc, inc in next sc] around. (36 sc)

ROUND 7: Working in **back loops** only, sc in each sc around. (36 sc)

ROUNDS 8-9: Working through both loops, sc in each sc around. (36 sc)

ROUND 10: [Sc in each of next 4 sc, sc-dec] 4 times, sc in each of next 12 sc. (32 sc)

ROUND 11: [Sc in each of next 3 sc, sc-dec] 4 times, sc in each of next 12 sc. (28 sc)

ROUND 12: [Sc in each of next 2 sc, sc-dec] 4 times, sc in each of next 12 sc, changing to Color A in last st. (24 sc) Cut Color B, leaving a long tail.

- Start stuffing the Legs, adding more as you go.

ROUNDS 13-25: Using Color A, sc in each sc around. (24 sc)

ROUND 26: [Sc in each of next 2 sc, sc-dec] 6 times. (18 sc) Fasten off Color A, leaving long tail for sewing.

- Finish stuffing the Legs firmly.
- Using Color A long tail and yarn needle, flatten last round and sew across 9 sts to close.
- Position Legs on either side of Body between Rounds 10 & 17 and sew in place.

- Using Color B long tails and yarn needle, repeat the paws as for Lion Arms.

TAIL

ROUND 1: (Right Side) Using Color A, make a Magic Ring, 6 sc in ring. DO NOT JOIN. (6 sc) Mark last stitch.

ROUND 2: *Sc in next sc, [inc in next sc] twice; rep from * once more. (10 sc) Move marker each round.

ROUNDS 3-30: Sc in each sc around. (10 sc) Leave another marker at the end of Round 3 (for Tail Tuft).

At the end of Round 30, fasten off leaving long tail for sewing.

- Stuff the Tail lightly.
- Using long tail and yarn needle, sew across last round (5 sts).
- Position Tail at back of Body between Legs (so that Lion can sit), and sew in place.

MANE

Using photo as guide, join Color C with sl st around post of any sc in front of Ear, work **Loop Stitches** (see Additional Stitches) all the way around face (in front of Ears). Continue working Loop Stitches until the entire back of Head is covered. When finished, work an additional sc to finish. Cut yarn and pull yarn end through loop. Weave in ends.

TAIL TUFT

Join Color C with sl st around post of marked sc on Round 3, work Loop Stitches in each stitch around towards tip of Tail. When finished, work an additional sc to finish. Cut yarn and pull yarn end through loop. Weave in ends.

Patchy Rabbit

By Dilek Yıldırım

MATERIALS NEEDED

DMC Natura Just Cotton
Color A - Ibiza (N01) for the Body and Limbs
Color B - Gerbera (N98) for Ears and Embroidery.

Hook
Size B-1 (2.25 mm) or size suitable for yarn used.

Other
Polyester Fiberfill for stuffing
⅜" (10 mm) Safety Eyes - 2
Cosmetic Blusher (optional)
2 Pieces of pink fabric about 1" (2.5 cm) by
1½" (4 cm) each - for cheeks
Piece of small bright fabric about
1½" (3.5 cm) square - for head patch
Black Embroidery Floss
Yarn Needle, sewing needle & thread,
scissors, stitch markers.

RABBIT

HEAD

ROUND 1: (Right Side) Using Color A, make a **Magic Ring** (see Techniques), 6 sc in ring. DO NOT JOIN. (6 sc) Mark last stitch.

ROUND 2: 2 sc in each sc around. (12 sc) Move marker each round.

ROUND 3: [Sc in next sc, **inc** (see Special Stitches) in next sc] around. (18 sc)

ROUND 4: [Sc in each of next 2 sc, inc in next sc] around. (24 sc)

ROUND 5: [Sc in each of next 3 sc, inc in next sc] around. (30 sc)

ROUND 6: [Sc in each of next 4 sc, inc in next sc] around. (36 sc)

ROUND 7: [Sc in each of next 5 sc, inc in next sc] around. (42 sc)

ROUND 8: [Sc in each of next 6 sc, inc in next sc] around. (48 sc)

ROUND 9: [Sc in each of next 7 sc, inc in next sc] around. (54 sc)

ROUND 10: [Sc in each of next 8 sc, inc in next sc] around. (60 sc)

ROUND 11: Sc in each sc around. (60 sc)

ROUND 12: [Sc in each of next 9 sc, inc in next sc] around. (66 sc)

ROUNDS 13-24: Sc in each sc around. (66 sc)

- Insert Safety Eyes between Rounds 19 & 20, with about 9 stitches between them.

- Stuff the Head as you go.

ROUND 25: [Sc in each of next 9 sc, **sc-dec** (see Special Stitches)] 6 times. (60 sc)

ROUND 26: [Sc in each of next 4 sc, sc-dec] 10 times. (50 sc)

ROUND 27: [Sc in each of next 3 sc, sc-dec] 10 times. (40 sc)

ROUND 28: [Sc in each of next 2 sc, sc-dec] 10 times. (30 sc)

ROUND 29: [Sc in each of next 3 sc, sc-dec] 6 times. (24 sc) Fasten off leaving a long tail for sewing.

- Stuff Head firmly.

- Using yarn needle and long tail, **close the opening** (see Techniques).

- Using Color B and yarn needle, embroider an "X" for the Nose and Mouth.

- Trim the corners of the 2 small pieces of fabric and position on either side of the Head as Cheeks. Using needle and thread, sew in place.

- Using the floss, embroider small stitches around the eyes to create an innocent expression.

EARS (Make 2)

ROUNDS 1-3: Using Color B, repeat Rounds 1-3 of Head. At the end of Round 3, there are 18 sc.

ROUNDS 4-5: Sc in each sc around. (18 sc)

ROUND 6: [Sc in each of next 2 sc, inc in next sc] around. (24 sc)

ROUNDS 7-11: Sc in each sc around. (24 sc)

ROUND 12: [Sc in each of next 2 sc, sc-dec] 6 times. (18 sc)

ROUNDS 13-15: Sc in each sc around. (18 sc)

ROUND 16: [Sc in next sc, sc-dec] 6 times. (12 sc)

ROUNDS 17-18: Sc in each sc around. (12 sc)

At the end of Round 18, fasten off leaving long tail for sewing. (Do not stuff the Ears.)

- Using long tail and yarn needle, position and sew Ears to Head.

- Cut the head patch fabric into a heart shape. Position on Head and sew in place.

BODY

ROUNDS 1-10: Using Color A, repeat Rounds 1-10 of Head. At the end of Round 10, there are 60 sc.

ROUNDS 11-15: Sc in each sc around. (60 sc)

ROUND 16: Sc in each of next 24 sc, [sc-dec] 6 times, sc in each of next 24 sc. (54 sc)

ROUND 17: Sc in each sc around. (54 sc)

ROUND 18: Sc in each of next 21 sc, [sc-dec] 6 times, sc in each of next 21 sc. (48 sc)

ROUND 19: Sc in each sc around. (48 sc)

ROUND 20: [Sc in each of next 6 sc, sc-dec] around. (42 sc)

ROUNDS 21-22: Sc in each sc around. (42 sc)

 - Start stuffing Body firmly.

ROUND 23: [Sc in each of next 5 sc, sc-dec] around. (36 sc)

ROUND 24: Sc in each sc around. (36 sc)

ROUND 25: [Sc in each of next 4 sc, sc-dec] around. (30 sc)

ROUND 26: Sc in each sc around. (30 sc)

ROUND 27: [Sc in each of next 3 sc, sc-dec] around. (24 sc)

ROUNDS 28-30: Sc in each sc around. (24 sc)

At the end of Round 30, fasten off leaving a long tail for sewing.

 - Using long tail and yarn needle, sew the Body to the second last round of Head, stuffing firmly before finishing.

ARMS (Make 2)

ROUNDS 1-3: Using Color A, repeat Rounds 1-3 of Head. At the end of Round 3, there are 18 sc.

ROUNDS 4-6: Sc in each sc around. (18 sc)

ROUND 7: [Sc in each of next 4 sc, sc-dec] 3 times. (15 sc)

ROUNDS 8-11: Sc in each sc around. (15 sc)

ROUND 12: Sc-dec, sc in each of next 13 sc. (14 sc)

ROUND 13: Sc in each sc around. (14 sc)

 - Start stuffing the Arms lightly, adding more as you go.

ROUND 14: Sc-dec, sc in each of next 12 sc. (13 sc)

ROUND 15: Sc in each sc around. (13 sc)

ROUND 16: Sc-dec, sc in each of next 11 sc. (12 sc)

ROUND 17: Sc in each sc around. (12 sc)

ROUND 18: Sc-dec, sc in each of next 10 sc. (11 sc)

ROUND 19: Sc in each sc around. (11 sc)

ROUND 20: Sc-dec, sc in each of next 9 sc. (10 sc)

ROUND 21: Sc in each sc around. (10 sc)
ROUND 22: Sc-dec, sc in each of next 8 sc. (9 sc)

ROUND 23: Sc in each sc around. (9 sc) Fasten off leaving long tail for sewing.

 - Finish stuffing the arms lightly.

 - Using long tail and yarn needle, flatten last round and sew across to close.

 - Position Arms on either side of Body at about Round 30 and sew in place.

LEGS (Make 2)

ROUNDS 1-7: Using Color A, repeat Rounds 1-7 of Head. At the end of Round 7, there are 42 sc.

ROUNDS 8-10: Sc in each sc around. (42 sc)

ROUND 11: Sc in each of next 15 sc, [sc-dec] 6 times, sc in each of next 15 sc. (36 sc)

ROUND 12: Sc in each of next 12 sc, [sc-dec] 6 times, sc in each of next 12 sc. (30 sc)

 - Start stuffing the Legs firmly, adding more as you go.

ROUND 13: [Sc in each of next 3 sc, sc-dec] around. (24 sc)

ROUND 14: Sc in each sc around. (24 sc)

ROUND 15: [Sc in each of next 2 sc, sc-dec] around. (18 sc)

ROUNDS 16-23: Sc in each sc around. (18 sc)

ROUND 24: [Sc in next sc, sc-dec] around. (12 sc) Fasten off leaving long tail for sewing.

 - Finish stuffing the Legs.

 - Using long tail and yarn needle, flatten last round and sew across 6 sts to close.

 - Position Legs on either side of Body between Rounds 9 & 13 and sew in place.

FEET PADS

Large Pad - make 2 (1 for each Foot)

ROUND 1: (Right Side) Using Color B, make a Magic Ring, 5 sc in ring. DO NOT JOIN. (5 sc) Mark last stitch.

ROUND 2: 2 sc in each sc around. (10 sc) Move marker each round.

ROUND 3: [Sc in next sc, inc in next sc] around. (15 sc) Fasten off using **Invisible Join** (see Techniques) and leaving a long tail for sewing.

Small Pads - make 6 (3 for each Foot)

ROUND 1: (Right Side) Using Color B, make a Magic Ring, 5 sc in ring. Fasten off using Invisible Join and leaving long tail for sewing

 - Using photo as guide, position and sew 1 Large Pad and 3 Small Pads to the sole of each foot.

EmmyLou The Doll

By Katerina Nikolaidau

FINISHED SIZE
About 10" (25,5 cm) tall.

MATERIALS NEEDED

DMC Natura Just Cotton
Color A – Ivory (N02) for skin
Color B – Bourgogne (N34) for Dress/Body and Shoes
Color C – Lobelia (N82) for Legs
Color D – Ibiza (N01) for Collar
Button Colors - Rose Soraya (N32), Erica (N51) &
Amaranto (N33)
Eye Color - Noir (N11)

DMC Woolly
Hair Color - Brown (113)

Hook
Size C-2 (2.75 mm) or size suitable for yarn used.

Other
Polyester Fiberfill for stuffing
Safety Eyes - 2 (optional)
Cosmetic Blusher (optional) for cheeks
Yarn Needle, sewing needle, scissors, stitch markers.

Designer's Tip
You can choose the colors for your doll's
skin, her hair and her clothes. You can also
style her hair any way you want.

DOLL

LEGS (Make 2)

ROUND 1: (Right Side) Using Color A, make a **Magic Ring** (see Techniques), 6 sc in ring. DO NOT JOIN. (6 sc) Mark last stitch.

ROUND 2: 2 sc in each sc around. (12 sc) Move marker each round.

ROUND 3: [Sc in next sc, **inc** (see Special Stitches) in next sc] around. (18 sc)

ROUND 4: [Sc in each of next 2 sc, inc in next sc] around. (24 sc)

ROUNDS 5-7: Sc in each sc around. (24 sc)

ROUND 8: [Sc in each of next 10 sc, **sc-dec** (see Special Stitches)] twice. (22 sc)

ROUND 9: Sc in each sc around. (22 sc)

- Start stuffing the Leg, adding more as you go.

ROUND 10: Sc in each of next 7 sc, [sc-dec] 4 times, sc in each of next 7 sc. (18 sc)

ROUND 11: Sc in each sc around. (18 sc)

ROUND 12: Sc in each of next 7 sc, [sc-dec] 3 times, sc in each of next 5 sc. (15 sc)

ROUND 13: Sc in each sc around. (15 sc)

ROUND 14: Sc in each of next 5 sc, [sc-dec] 3 times, sc in each of next 4 sc. (12 sc)

ROUNDS 15-19: Sc in each sc around. (12 sc) At the end of Round 19, **change color** (see Techniques) to Color C. Cut Color A and weave in ends.

ROUNDS 20-36: With Color C, sc in each sc around. (12 sc) At the end of Round 36, fasten off with **Invisible Join** (see Techniques). Do not close top of Leg. Weave in ends.

- Finish stuffing the Legs.

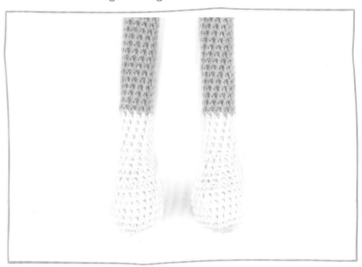

DRESS / BODY

FOUNDATION ROW: Using Color B, ch 6, pick up the first Leg (with foot facing forward), fold last round flat and working through both thicknesses, sc in each of next 6 sc (the leg is now closed), ch 6, pick up next Leg with foot facing forward, fold last round flat and working through both thicknesses, sc in each of next 6 sc, ch 7. (31 sts – 19 ch & 12 sc)

ROUND 1: Working in the **front loops** only (see Techniques) of all stitches, sc in 2nd ch from hook, sc in each of next 29 sts, working along other side of starting chain, in **back loops** only (see Techniques), sc in each of next 30 sts. DO NOT JOIN. (60 sc) Mark last stitch.

ROUND 2: Working in a spiral, [sc-dec, sc in each of next 26 sc, sc-dec] twice. (56 sc) Move marker each round.

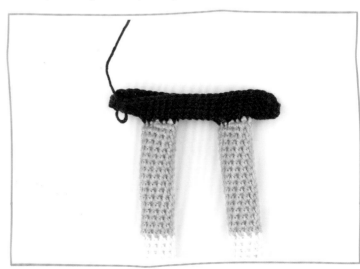

ROUND 3: [Sc-dec, sc in each of next 24 sc, sc-dec] twice. (52 sc)

ROUND 4: Sc in each sc around. (52 sc)

ROUND 5: [Sc-dec, sc in each of next 22 sc, sc-dec] twice. (48 sc)

ROUNDS 6-7: Sc in each sc around. (48 sc)

ROUND 8: [Sc-dec, sc in each of next 20 sc, sc-dec] twice. (44 sc)

ROUND 9: [Sc-dec, sc in each of next 18 sc, sc-dec] twice. (40 sc)

ROUNDS 10-11: Sc in each sc around. (40 sc)

ROUND 12: [Sc-dec, sc in each of next 16 sc, sc-dec] twice. (36 sc)

ROUNDS 13-14: Sc in each sc around. (36 sc)

- Start stuffing the Dress/Body firmly, adding more as you go.

ROUND 15: [Sc in each of next 5 sc, sc-dec] 5 times, sc in last sc. (31 sc)

ROUND 16: Sc in each sc around. (31 sc)

ROUND 17: Sc in each of next 9 sc, sc-dec, [sc in each of next 8 sc, sc-dec] twice. (28 sc)

ROUND 18: Sc in each sc around. (28 sc)

ROUND 19: [Sc in each of next 5 sc, sc-dec] 4 times. (24 sc)

ROUND 20: [Sc in each of next 4 sc, sc-dec] 4 times. (20 sc)

ROUND 21: Sc in each sc around. (20 sc)

ROUND 22: [Sc in each of next 3 sc, sc-dec] 4 times. (16 sc)

ROUND 23: Sc in each sc around, changing color to Color A in last st. (16 sc) Cut Color B and weave in ends. Do not close top of Body.

- Finish stuffing the Dress/Body.

HEAD

ROUND 1: Continuing from Dress/Body, using Color A, [sc in next sc, inc in next sc] 8 times. (24 sc)

ROUND 2: [Sc in each of next 2 sc, inc in next sc] 8 times. (32 sc)

ROUND 3: [Sc in each of next 3 sc, inc in next sc] 8 times. (40 sc)

ROUND 4: [Sc in each of next 4 sc, inc in next sc] 8 times. (48 sc)

ROUNDS 5-19: Sc in each sc around. (48 sc)
At the end of Round 19, DO NOT FASTEN OFF.

- Using the Eye Color, embroider the eyes (or insert Safety Eyes) between Rounds 10 & 11, with about 9-10 stitches between them.

- Using Color A, working two rounds below the Eyes, embroider the Nose using a **Bullion Stitch** (see Embroidery) between the Eyes.

- Using Color A, embroider the Mouth between Rounds 5 & 6, using straight stitches across 3 sc-sts.

- Apply a little blusher to the cheeks.

- Stuff the Neck firmly.

ROUND 20: [Sc in each of next 4 sc, sc-dec] 8 times. (40 sc)

- Start stuffing the Head, adding more as you go.

ROUND 21: [Sc in each of next 3 sc, sc-dec] 8 times. (32 sc)

ROUND 22: [Sc in each of next 2 sc, sc-dec] 8 times. (24 sc)

ROUND 23-24: [Sc in next sc, sc-dec] 8 times. (16 sc)

ROUND 25: [Sc-dec] 8 times. (8 sc) Fasten off leaving long tail for sewing.

- Finish stuffing the Head.

- Using tail and yarn needle, **close the opening** (see Techniques).

ARMS (Make 2)

ROUND 1: (Right Side) Using Color A, make a Magic Ring, 5 sc in ring. DO NOT JOIN. (6 sc) Mark last stitch.

ROUND 2: 2 sc in each sc around. (10 sc) Move marker each round.

ROUND 3: [Sc in each of next 4 sc, inc in next sc] twice. (12 sc)

ROUNDS 4-5: Sc in each sc around. (12 sc)

ROUND 6: [Sc in each of next 4 sc, sc-dec] twice. (10 sc)

ROUNDS 7-8: Sc in each sc around. (10 sc)
At the end of Round 8, change color to Color B. Cut Color A and weave in ends.

- Stuff the Hand only. Do not stuff the rest of the Arm.

ROUNDS 9-26: Using Color B, sc in each sc around. (10 sc)

At the end of Round 26, ch 1, fold last round flat, and working through both thicknesses, sc in each of next 5 sc (to close the Arms). Fasten off leaving long tail for sewing Arms to Body.

- Using photo as guide, position and sew Arms to either side of Body.

COLLAR

ROW 1: (Right Side) Using Color D, ch 22, dc in 2ⁿᵈ ch from hook, 2 dc in next ch, [dc in next ch, 2 dc in next ch] 4 times, (dc, hdc) in next ch, ch 1, sl st in next ch, ch 1, (hdc, dc) in next ch, [dc in next ch, 2 dc in next ch] 4 times. Fasten off leaving long tail to sew Collar to Body.

- Using photo as guide, position and sew Collar around Neck.

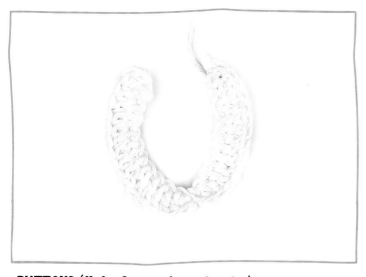

BUTTONS (Make 3 – one in each color)

ROUND 1: (Right Side) Using Button Color, starting with a long tail, make a Magic Ring, 6 sc in ring. Fasten off using Invisible Join.

- Tug the long starting tail to close the Magic Ring. Using yarn needle secure the Magic Ring and using photo as guide, sew Buttons onto front of Dress.

SHOES (Make 2)

ROUNDS 1-8: Using Color B, repeat Rounds 1-8 of Legs. After Round 8, there are 22 sc.

Work continues in Rows.

ROW 9: Sc in each of next 14 sc. (14 sc) Leave remaining sts unworked.

ROW 10: Ch 1, turn, sc in each of next 14 sc. (14 sc) Leave remaining sts unworked.

ROWS 11-13: Ch 1, turn, sc in each sc across (14 sc)

ROW 14: Ch 1, (do NOT turn), working in sides of rows, sc in each of next 4 rows, sc in same st as last sc on Row 9, working in unused sts on Round 8, sc in each of next 8 sc, sc in same sc as last sc on Row 10, working in sides of rows, sc in each of next 3 rows, sl st in first sc on Row 13, ch 7, turn, skip next 17 sc; join with sl st to ch-1 sp. Fasten off using Invisible Join.

WIG

ROUND 1: (Right Side) Using Hair Color, make a Magic Ring, 8 sc in ring. DO NOT JOIN. (8 sc) Mark last stitch.

ROUND 2: 2 sc in each sc around. (16 sc) Move marker each round.

ROUND 3: [Sc in next sc, inc in next sc] around. (24 sc)

ROUND 4: [Sc in each of next 2 sc, inc in next sc] around. (32 sc)

ROUND 5: [Sc in each of next 3 sc, inc in next sc] around. (40 sc)

ROUND 6: [Sc in each of next 4 sc, inc in next sc] around. (48 sc)

ROUNDS 7-15: Sc in each sc around. (48 sc)
After Round 15, work continues in Rows.

ROW 16: Ch 1, turn, sc in each of next 48 sc. (48 sc)

ROW 17: Ch 1, turn, sc-dec, sc in each of next 44 sc, sc-dec. (46 sc)

ROW 18: Ch 1, turn, sc-dec, sc in each of next 42 sc, sc-dec. (44 sc)

ROW 19: Ch 1, turn, sc-dec, sc in each of next 40 sc, sc-dec. (42 sc) Fasten off, leaving a long tail to sew Wig to Head.

- Using photo as guide, position Wig on Head and using long tail, sew in place. Before fastening off, sew a few long stitches to resemble bangs (hair fringe).

BRAIDS (Make 2)

Using Hair Color, make a Magic Ring, *ch 41, sl st in 2nd ch from hook, [sl st in next ch] across (40 sl sts), sl st in magic ring; repeat from * 7 times more. (8 strands)

- Tug the starting tail to close the Magic Ring. Using yarn needle secure the Magic Ring.

- Using photo as guide, position and attach Braids to either side of Wig.

BOW

Holding one strand of Color B and one strand of Color C together, leaving a long tail, ch 5, (3 tr, sl st, ch 4, 3 tr, sl st) in 5th ch from hook. Leaving a long tail, cut yarn. Wrap the beginning and end yarn tails around the center of the Bow a few times and secure with a knot on the wrong side.

- Using photo as guide, position and attach the Bow to the one Braid.

Cutie The Bunny

By Katerina Nikolaidau

FINISHED SIZE
About 11½" (29 cm) tall

MATERIALS NEEDED

DMC Natura Just Cotton
Color A - Ivory (N02)
Color B - Coral (N18) for Dress
Color C - Ble (N83) for Bow/Headband
Flower Colors - Tournesol (N16) & Bourgogne (N34)
Eye Color - Noir (N11)
Nose Color - Rose Layette (N06)

DMC Woolly
Tail Color - Cream (03)

Hook
Size C-2 (2.75 mm) or size suitable for yarn used.

Other
Polyester Fiberfill for stuffing
Safety Eyes - 2 (optional)
Cosmetic Blusher (optional)
Yarn Needle, sewing needle, scissors, stitch markers.

Designer's Tip
You can choose the colors for your bunny's body, dress and flowers. You can also choose whether you want a bow or a headband for the head.

BUNNY

LEGS (Make 2)

ROUND 1: (Right Side) Using Color A, make a **Magic Ring** (see Techniques), 6 sc in ring. DO NOT JOIN. (6 sc) Mark last stitch.

ROUND 2: 2 sc in each sc around. (12 sc) Move marker each round.

ROUND 3: [Sc in next sc, **inc** (see Special Stitches) in next sc] around. (18 sc)

ROUND 4: [Sc in each of next 2 sc, inc in next sc] around. (24 sc)

ROUNDS 5-8: Sc in each sc around. (24 sc)

ROUND 9: [Sc in each of next 2 sc, **sc-dec** (see Special Stitches)] 6 times. (18 sc)

ROUND 10: [Sc in next sc, sc-dec] 6 times. (12 sc)

ROUNDS 11-35: Sc in each sc around. (12 sc)

At the end of Round 35, fasten off with **Invisible Join** (see Techniques) and weave in ends.

- Stuff each Leg and set aside.

DRESS

FOUNDATION ROW: Using Color B, ch 6, pick up the first Leg (with foot facing forward), fold last round flat and working through both thicknesses, sc in each of next 6 sc (the leg is now closed), ch 6, pick up next Leg with foot facing forward, fold last round flat and working through both thicknesses, sc in each of next 6 sc, ch 7. (31 sts – 19 ch & 12 sc)

Please refer to "EmmyLou The Doll" project between the pages 78 - 83 for the step-by-step images of this project.

ROUND 1: Working in the **front loops** only (see Techniques) of all stitches, sc in 2nd ch from hook, sc in each of next 29 sts, working along other side of starting chain, in **back loops** only (see Techniques), sc in each of next 30 sts. DO NOT JOIN. (60 sc) Mark last stitch.

ROUND 2: Working in a spiral, [sc-dec, sc in each of next 26 sc, sc-dec] twice. (56 sc) Move marker each round.

ROUND 3: [Sc-dec, sc in each of next 24 sc, sc-dec] twice. (52 sc)

ROUND 4: Sc in each sc around. (52 sc)

ROUND 5: [Sc-dec, sc in each of next 22 sc, sc-dec] twice. (48 sc)

ROUNDS 6-7: Sc in each sc around. (48 sc)

ROUND 8: [Sc-dec, sc in each of next 20 sc, sc-dec] twice. (44 sc)

ROUND 9: [Sc-dec, sc in each of next 18 sc, sc-dec] twice. (40 sc)

ROUNDS 10-11: Sc in each sc around. (40 sc)

ROUND 12: [Sc-dec, sc in each of next 16 sc, sc-dec] twice. (36 sc)

ROUNDS 13-14: Sc in each sc around. (36 sc)

- Start stuffing the Dress/Body firmly, adding more as you go.

ROUND 15: [Sc in each of next 5 sc, sc-dec] 5 times, sc in last sc. (31 sc)

ROUND 16: Sc in each sc around. (31 sc)

ROUND 17: Sc in each of next 9 sc, sc-dec, [sc in each of next 8 sc, sc-dec] twice. (28 sc)

ROUND 18: Sc in each sc around. (28 sc)

ROUND 19: [Sc in each of next 5 sc, sc-dec] 4 times. (24 sc)

ROUND 20: [Sc in each of next 4 sc, sc-dec] 4 times. (20 sc)

ROUND 21: Sc in each sc around. (20 sc)

ROUND 22: [Sc in each of next 3 sc, sc-dec] 4 times. (16 sc)

ROUND 23: Sc in each sc around, changing color to Color A in last st. (16 sc) Cut Color B and weave in ends. Do not close top of Body.

- Finish stuffing the Dress firmly.

HEAD

ROUND 1: Continuing from Dress, using Color A, [sc in next sc, inc in next sc] 8 times. (24 sc)

ROUND 2: [Sc in each of next 2 sc, inc in next sc] 8 times. (32 sc)

ROUND 3: [Sc in each of next 3 sc, inc in next sc] 8 times. (40 sc)

ROUND 4: [Sc in each of next 4 sc, inc in next sc] 8 times. (48 sc)

ROUNDS 5-19: Sc in each sc around. (48 sc)
At the end of Round 19, DO NOT FASTEN OFF.

- Embroider the eyes (or insert Safety Eyes) between Rounds 11 & 12, with about 9-10 stitches between them.

- Using Nose Color, embroider an "X" for the Nose and Mouth.

- Apply a little Blusher to the cheeks.

- Stuff the Neck firmly.

ROUND 20: [Sc in each of next 4 sc, sc-dec] 8 times. (40 sc)

- Start stuffing the Head, adding more as you go.

ROUND 21: [Sc in each of next 3 sc, sc-dec] 8 times. (32 sc)

ROUND 22: [Sc in each of next 2 sc, sc-dec] 8 times. (24 sc)

ROUND 23: [Sc in next sc, sc-dec] 8 times. (16 sc)

ROUND 24: [Sc-dec] 8 times. (8 sc) Fasten off leaving long tail for sewing.

- Finish stuffing the Head.

- Using tail and yarn needle, **close the opening** (see Techniques).

EARS (Make 2)

ROUND 1: (Right Side) Using Color A, make a Magic Ring, 5 sc in ring. DO NOT JOIN. (6 sc) Mark last stitch.

ROUND 2: 2 sc in each sc around. (10 sc) Move marker each round.

ROUND 3: [Sc in each of next 4 sc, inc in next sc] twice. (12 sc)

ROUND 4: [Sc in each of next 5 sc, inc in next sc] twice. (14 sc)

ROUND 5: [Sc in each of next 6 sc, inc in next sc] twice. (16 sc)

ROUND 6: [Sc in each of next 7 sc, inc in next sc] twice. (18 sc)

ROUNDS 7-9: Sc in each sc around. (18 sc)
ROUND 10: [Sc in each of next 7 sc, sc-dec] twice. (16 sc)
ROUNDS 11-12: Sc in each sc around. (16 sc)

ROUND 13: [Sc in each of next 6 sc, sc-dec] twice. (14 sc)

ROUND 14: Sc in each sc around. (14 sc)

ROUND 15: [Sc in each of next 5 sc, sc-dec] twice. (12 sc) Fasten off leaving long tail.

- Flatten Ear and using yarn needle and long tail, sew across the last round (6 sts).

- Position and sew Ears to top of Head.

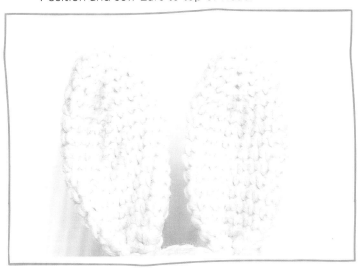

ARMS (Make 2)

ROUND 1: (Right Side) Using Color A, make a Magic Ring, 6 sc in ring. DO NOT JOIN. (6 sc) Mark last stitch.

ROUND 2: 2 sc in each sc around. (12 sc) Move marker each round.

ROUND 3: [Sc in next sc, inc in next sc] 6 times. (18 sc)

ROUNDS 4-5: Sc in each sc around. (18 sc)

ROUND 6: [Sc in next sc, sc-dec] 6 times. (12 sc)

ROUND 7: [Sc in each of next 4 sc, sc-dec] twice. (10 sc)

ROUNDS 8-9: Sc in each sc around. (10 sc)
At the end of Round 9, **change color** (see Techniques) to Color B. Cut Color A and weave in ends.

- Stuff the Hand only. Do not stuff the rest of the arm.

ROUNDS 10-26: Using Color B, sc in each sc around. (10 sc)
At the end of Round 26, ch 1, fold last round flat, and working through both thicknesses, sc in each of next 5 sc (to close the Arms). Fasten off leaving long tail for sewing Arms to Body.

- Using photo as guide, using yarn needle and long tail, position and sew Arms to either side of Body.

TAIL

ROUND 1: (Right Side) Using Tail Color, make a Magic Ring, 6 sc in ring. DO NOT JOIN. (6 sc) Mark last stitch.
ROUND 2: 2 sc in each sc around. (12 sc) Move marker each round.

ROUND 3: [Sc in next sc, inc in next sc] 6 times. (18 sc)

ROUND 4: [Sc in next sc, sc-dec] 6 times. (12 sc)

ROUND 5: [Sc-dec] 6 times. (6 sc) Fasten off leaving long tail for sewing.

- Stuff the tail with a small amount of Fiberfill.

- Position the Tail at the back of the Body and using long tail and yarn needle, sew in place.

BOW

ROUND 1: (Right Side) Using Color C, ch 24; taking care not to twist chain, join with sl st to first ch to form a ring; ch 1, sc in same st as joining, [sc in next ch] around; join with sl st to first sc. (24 sc)

ROUNDS 2-5: Ch 1, sc in each sc around; join with sl st to first sc. (24 sc)
At the end of Round 5, fasten off leaving long tail.

- Fold the ring and wrap the long tail a few times around the center of the Bow. Knot the tails together on the wrong side. (Alternatively, wrap Color B around center of Bow.)

- Position and sew Bow to front of Bunny's Neck.

HEADBAND

ROW 1: Using color C, ch 3, sc in 2nd ch from hook, sc in last ch. (2 sc)

ROW 2: Ch 1, turn, sc in each sc across (2 sc)

Repeat Row 2 to desired length to fit around Bunny's Head. Fasten off.

- Using yarn needle, sew last round to first round to form the Headband.

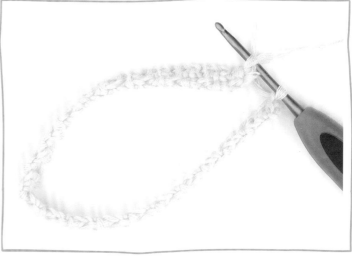

FLOWER – (Make 3 – Use Photo As Guide For Colors)

ROUND 1: (Right Side) Using the first Flower Color, make a Magic Ring, 5 sc in ring, changing to next Flower Color in last stitch; join with sl st to first sc. Cut first color.

ROUND 2: Ch 2, 3 hdc in same st as joining, [(sl st, ch 2, 3 hdc) in next sc] 4 times, sl st in next sc. (5 petals) Fasten off leaving long tail.

- Close and secure the magic rings.

- Using photo as guide, using long tails and yarn needle, sew one Flower onto Headband. Sew the remaining two Flowers together and sew them on front of Dress.

Blackberry Doll

By Tatyana Korobkova

FINISHED SIZE
About 13¾" (35 cm) tall.

MATERIALS NEEDED

DMC Natura Just Cotton
Color A - Nacar (N35) - for Head / Arms
Color B - Prusian (N64) for Hair
Color C - Rose Layette (N06) - for Dress/Ruffle
Color D - Nacar (N35) - Neck
Color E - Ibiza (N01) - for Dress Edging & Socks
Color F - Azur (N56) - for Hat/Coat
Color G - Glacier (N87) - Coat Edging/Hat Edging
Color H - Canelle (N37) - for Legs
Color I - Crimson (N61) – for Socks/ Scarf
Color J - Light Green (N12) - for Ball on Hat

Hook
Size C-2 (2.75 mm) or size suitable for yarn used.

Other
Polyester Fiberfill for stuffing
8mm x 6mm Oval Safety Eyes - 2
Cosmetic Blusher for Cheeks
Yarn Needle, sewing needle, pins, scissors, stitch markers.

DOLL

HEAD

ROUND 1: (Right Side) Using Color A, make a **Magic Ring** (see Techniques), 6 sc in ring. DO NOT JOIN. (6 sc) Mark last stitch.

ROUND 2: 2 sc in each sc around. (12 sc) Move marker each round.

ROUND 3: [Sc in next sc, **inc** (see Special Stitches) in next sc] around. (18 sc)

ROUND 4: [Sc in each of next 2 sc, inc in next sc] around. (24 sc)

ROUND 5: [Sc in each of next 3 sc, inc in next sc] around. (30 sc)

ROUND 6: [Sc in each of next 4 sc, inc in next sc] around. (36 sc)

ROUND 7: [Sc in each of next 5 sc, inc in next sc] around. (42 sc)

ROUND 8: [Sc in each of next 6 sc, inc in next sc] around. (48 sc)

ROUNDS 9-10: Sc in each sc around. (48 sc)

ROUND 11: [Sc in each of next 7 sc, inc in next sc] around. (54 sc)

ROUNDS 12-25: Sc in each sc around. (54 sc)

- Insert Safety Eyes between Rounds 19&20

ROUND 26: [Sc in each of next 7 sc, **sc-dec** (see Special Stitches)] around. (48 sc)

ROUND 27: [Sc in each of next 6 sc, sc-dec] around. (42 sc)

ROUND 28: [Sc in each of next 5 sc, sc-dec] around. (36 sc)

ROUND 29: [Sc in each of next 4 sc, sc-dec] around. (30 sc)

- Start stuffing Head firmly, adding more as you go.

ROUND 30: [Sc in each of next 3 sc, sc-dec] around. (24 sc)

ROUND 31: [Sc in each of next 2 sc, sc-dec] around. (18 sc)

ROUND 32: [Sc in next sc, sc-dec] around. (12 sc)

ROUND 33: [Sc-dec] around. (6 sc) Fasten off leaving long tail for sewing.

- Finish stuffing Head.

- Using yarn needle and long tail, **close the opening** (see Techniques).

HAIR

ROW 1: (Right Side) Using Color B, starting with a long tail, ch 37, sc in 2nd ch from hook, [sc in next ch] across. (36 sc)

ROWS 2-42: Ch 1, turn, working in **back loops** only (see Techniques), sc in each sc across. (36 sc)

ROW 43: Ch 1, turn, working in **back loops** only, sc in first sc, sc in each of next 17 sc. (18 sc)

ROWS 44-59: Ch 1, turn, working in **back loops** only, sc in each sc across. (18 sc)

At the end of Row 59, fasten off leaving long tail for sewing.

Using end tail and yarn needle, matching stitches, sew last row to first 18 sts of starting chain to form a tube. Do not fasten off and remove needle.

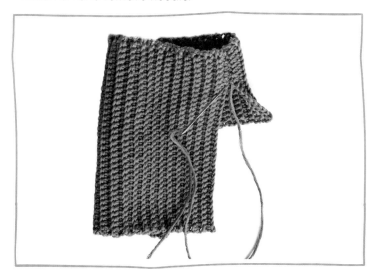

Using starting tail and yarn needle, gather stitches around top of Hair, pull to tighten and secure with a knot. Fasten off and weave in all ends.

Position Hair on Head and using end tail and yarn needle, tack in place.

- Apply a little blusher to the cheeks.

BODY / DRESS

ROUNDS 1-8: Using Color C, repeat Rounds 1-8 of Head. At the end of Round 8, there are 48 sc.

ROUND 9: [Sc in each of next 7 sc, inc in next sc] around. (54 sc)

ROUND 10: Working in **back loops** only, sc in each sc around. (54 sc)

ROUNDS 11-13: Working in both loops, sc in each sc around. (54 sc)

ROUND 14: [Sc in each of next 7 sc, sc-dec] around. (48 sc)

ROUNDS 15-17: Sc in each sc around. (48 sc)

ROUND 18: [Sc in each of next 6 sc, sc-dec] around. (42 sc)

ROUNDS 19-22: Sc in each sc around. (42 sc)

ROUND 23: [Sc in each of next 5 sc, sc-dec] around. (36 sc)

ROUNDS 24-28: Sc in each sc around. (36 sc)

- Start stuffing Body firmly, adding more as you go.

ROUND 29: [Sc in each of next 4 sc, sc-dec] around. (30 sc)

ROUNDS 30-32: Sc in each sc around. (30 sc)

ROUND 33: [Sc in each of next 3 sc, sc-dec] around. (24 sc)

ROUNDS 34-36: Sc in each sc around. (24 sc)

ROUND 37: [Sc in each of next 2 sc, sc-dec] around. (18 sc)

ROUND 38: [Sc in each of next 4 sc, sc-dec] 3 times, **changing color** (see Techniques) to Color D. (15 sc) Cut Color C.

ROUNDS 39-41: (Neck) With Color D, sc in each sc around. (15 sc) At the end of Round 41, fasten off leaving long tail for sewing.

Dress Ruffle

ROUND 1: With right side of Body/Dress facing, with Neck pointing downwards, working in unused front loops on Round 9, using Color C, **join with sc** (see Techniques) to any front loop, [sc in next front loop around; join with sl st to first sc. (54 sc)

ROUND 2: Ch 3 (counts as first dc, now and throughout), dc in same st as joining, [2 dc in next sc] around; join with sl st to first dc (3rd ch of beg ch-3). (108 dc)

ROUND 3: Ch 3, dc in same st as joining, dc in next dc, [2 dc in next dc, dc in next dc] around; join with sl st to first dc (3rd ch of beg ch-3). (162 dc)

ROUND 4: Ch 3, [dc in next dc] around, changing to Color E in last st; with Color E, join with sl st to first dc (3rd ch of beg ch-3). (162 dc)

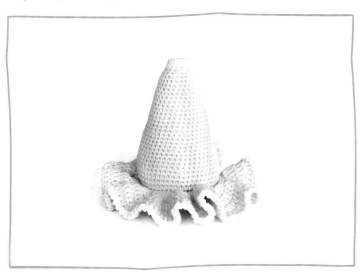

Edging Round: With Color E, [ch 1, sl st in next dc] around. (162 sl sts & 162 ch-1 sps) Fasten off and weave in all ends.

- Finish stuffing Body and using long tail and yarn needle, sew to Head.

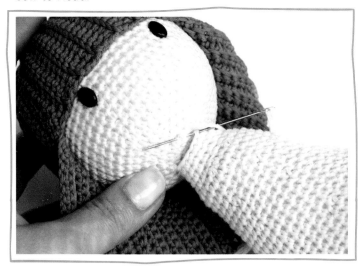

COAT

ROW 1: (Right Side) Using Color F, ch 26, dc in 4th ch from hook (skipped ch count as first dc), [dc in next ch] across. (24 dc)

ROW 2: Ch 3 (counts as first dc, now and throughout), turn, dc in each of next 2 dc, 2 dc in next dc, dc in each of next 16 dc, 2 dc in next dc, dc in each of last 3 dc. (26 dc)

ROW 3: Ch 3, turn, dc in each of next 2 dc, 2 dc in next dc, dc in each of next 18 dc, 2 dc in next dc, dc in each of last 3 dc. (28 dc)

ROW 4: Ch 3, turn, dc in each of next 2 dc, 2 dc in next dc, dc in each of next 20 dc, 2 dc in next dc, dc in each of last 3 dc. (30 dc)

ROW 5: Ch 3, turn, dc in each of next 2 dc, 2 dc in next dc, dc in each of next 22 dc, 2 dc in next dc, dc in each of last 3 dc. (32 dc)

ROW 6: Ch 3, turn, dc in each of next 2 dc, 2 dc in next dc, dc in each of next 24 dc, 2 dc in next dc, dc in each of last 3 dc. (34 dc)

ROW 7: Ch 3, turn, dc in each of next 2 dc, 2 dc in next dc, dc in each of next 26 dc, 2 dc in next dc, dc in each of last 3 dc. (36 dc)

ROW 8: Ch 3, turn, dc in each of next 2 dc, 2 dc in next dc, dc in each of next 28 dc, 2 dc in next dc, dc in each of last 3 dc. (38 dc)

ROW 9: Ch 3, turn, dc in each of next 2 dc, 2 dc in next dc, dc in each of next 30 dc, 2 dc in next dc, dc in each of last 3 dc. (40 dc)

ROW 10: Ch 3, turn, dc in each of next 2 dc, 2 dc in next dc, dc in each of next 32 dc, 2 dc in next dc, dc in each of last 3 dc. (42 dc)

ROW 11: Ch 3, turn, dc in each of next 2 dc, 2 dc in next dc, dc in each of next 34 dc, 2 dc in next dc, dc in each of last 3 dc. (44 dc)

ROW 12: Ch 3, turn, 2 dc in next dc, [dc in next dc, 2 dc in next dc] across. (66 dc)

ROW 13: Ch 3, turn, dc in next dc, 2 dc in next dc, [dc in each of next 2 dc, 2 dc in next dc] across. (88 dc) Fasten off and weave in all ends.

Edging Round: With right side facing, using Color G, working in Row 13, join with sl st to first dc, [ch 1, sl st in next dc] across, working in sides of rows, evenly work [ch 1, sl st] across; working in unused loops on other side of starting chain, [ch 1, sl st] in next ch across; working in sides of rows, [ch 1, sl st] evenly across. Fasten off and weave in all ends.

Position the Coat on the Body and secure it with pins.

Coat Sleeves

ROUND 1: (Right Side) Using Color F, starting with long tail, make a Magic Ring, 10 sc in ring; join with sl st to first sc. (10 sc)

ROUND 2: Ch 1 (does NOT count as first st), dc in first sc, [dc in next sc] around; join with sl st to first dc. (10 dc)

ROUNDS 3-9: Ch 1, dc in first dc, [dc in next dc] around; join with sl st to first dc. (10 dc)

ROUND 10: Ch 1, 2 dc in first dc, [2 dc in next dc] around, changing to Color G in last st; with Color G, join with sl st to first dc. (20 dc)

Edging Row: With Color G, [ch 1, sl st in next dc] around. (20 sl sts & 20 ch-1 sps) Fasten off and weave in all ends.

ARMS (make 2)

ROUND 1: (Right Side) Using Color A, leaving long tail on right side, make a Magic Ring, 8 sc in ring. DO NOT JOIN. (8 sc) Mark last stitch.

ROUNDS 2-25: Sc in each sc around. (8 sc) Move marker each round.

At the end of Round 25, fasten off leaving long tail for sewing.

- Using yarn needle and long tail, **close the opening** (see Techniques) and weave in end.

Insert Arms into Sleeves (using starting tail and yarn needle), and sew to Body (through Coat).

LEGS (make 2)

ROUND 1: (Right Side) Using Color H, leaving long tail on right side, make a Magic Ring, 6 sc in ring. DO NOT JOIN. (6 sc) Mark last stitch.

ROUND 2: 2 sc in each sc around. (12 sc) Move marker each round.

ROUND 3: [Sc in each of next 3 sc, inc in next sc] 3 times. (15 sc)

ROUNDS 4-10: Sc in each sc around. (15 sc)

- Remove hook and flatten piece. Using a separate strand of Color H and yarn needle, stitch through both thicknesses across Round 9 to create an unstuffed piece for attaching to Body.

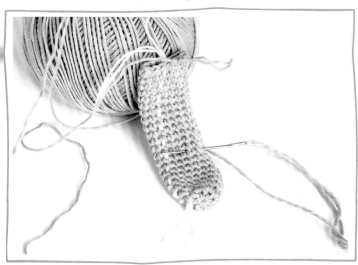

ROUNDS 11-24: Sc in each sc around. (15 sc)
At the end of Round 24, **change color** (see Techniques) to Color I in last stitch. Cut Color H.

- Start stuffing Leg firmly, adding as you go.

ROUNDS 25-29: With Color I, sc in each sc around. (15 sc)
At the end of Round 29, change to Color E in last stitch.

ROUNDS 30-32: With Color E, sc in each sc around. (15 sc)
At the end of Round 32, change to Color I in last stitch.

ROUNDS 33-35: With Color I, sc in each sc around. (15 sc)
At the end of Round 35, change to Color E in last stitch.

ROUNDS 36-38: With Color E, sc in each sc around. (15 sc)
At the end of Round 38, change to Color I in last stitch. Cut Color E.

ROUNDS 39-51: With Color I, sc in each sc around. (15 sc)

ROUND 52: [Sc in each of next 3 sc, sc-dec] around. (12 sc)

ROUND 53: [Sc-dec] around. (6 sc) Fasten off leaving long tail for sewing.

- Finish stuffing Leg.
- Using yarn needle and long tail, **close the opening** (see Techniques) and weave in end.

Position Legs to bottom of Body.

- Using starting tail and yarn needle, sew in place.

HAT

ROUNDS 1-8: Using Color F, repeat Rounds 1-8 of Head. At the end of Round 8, there are 48 sc.

ROUND 9: [Sc in each of next 7 sc, inc in next sc] around. (54 sc)

ROUND 10: [Sc in each of next 8 sc, inc in next sc] around. (60 sc)

ROUND 11: [Sc in each of next 9 sc, inc in next sc] around. (66 sc)

ROUNDS 12-20: Sc in each sc around. (66 sc)

ROUND 21: [Sc in each of next 21 sc, inc in next sc] around, changing to Color G in last st. (69 sc)

ROUNDS 22-24: With Color G, sc in each sc around. (69 sc) At the end of Round 24, change to Color C in last st.

ROUND 25: With Color C, sc in each sc around, sl st in next st. (69 sc) Fasten off and weave in all ends.

Large Ball

ROUND 1: (Right Side) Using Color I, make a Magic Ring, 6 sc in ring. DO NOT JOIN. (6 sc)

ROUND 2: 2 sc in each sc around. (12 sc)

ROUND 3: Sc in each sc around. (12 sc)

ROUND 4: [Sc-dec] around. (6 sc) Fasten off leaving long tail for sewing.

- Stuff ball firmly.

Medium Ball

ROUND 1: (Right Side) Using Color J, make a Magic Ring, 4 sc in ring. DO NOT JOIN. (4 sc)

ROUND 2: 2 sc in each sc around. (8 sc)

ROUND 3: Sc in each sc around. (8 sc)

ROUND 4: [Sc-dec] around. (4 sc) Fasten off leaving long tail for sewing.

- Stuff ball firmly.

Small Ball

ROUND 1: (Right Side) Using Color C, make a Magic Ring, 3 sc in ring. DO NOT JOIN. (3 sc)

ROUND 2: 2 sc in each sc around. (6 sc)

ROUND 3: Sc in each sc around. (6 sc)

ROUND 4: [Sc-dec] around. (3 sc) Fasten off leaving long tail for sewing.

- Stuff ball firmly.

Using long tails and yarn needle, position and sew Balls to Hat.

SCARF

ROW 1: (Right Side) Using Color I, ch 101, sc in 2nd ch from hook, [sc in next ch] across. (100 sc)

ROWS 2-4: Ch 1, turn, sc in each sc across. (100 sc) At the end of Row 4, Fasten off and weave in all ends.

- Wrap the Scarf around the Neck of Doll.

Waldorf Bunnies

By Tatyana Korobkova

FINISHED SIZE
Small Bunny-about 7" (18cm) tall
Medium Bunny-about 11" (28cm) tall
Large Bunny-about 15" (38cm) tall

MATERIALS NEEDED

For Small Bunny
DMC Natura Just Cotton
Color A - Nacar (N35) - for Head
Color B - Rose Soraya (N32)
Color C - Light Green (N12) (optional) - for Hat Edging

For Medium Bunny
DMC Natura Just Cotton Medium
Color A - Natural (#03) - for Head
Color B - Blue Bliss (#07)

For Large Bunny
DMC Natura Just Cotton XL
Color A - Natural (#03) - for Head
Color B - Aqua (#73)

Hook
For Small Bunny - Size C-2 (2.75 mm) or size suitable for yarn used.
For Medium Bunny - Size D-3 (3.25 mm) or size suitable for yarn used.
For Large Bunny - Size F-5 (3.75 mm) or size suitable for yarn used.

Other
Polyester Fiberfill for stuffing
Safety Eyes - 2 per bunny
Cosmetic Blusher for Cheeks
Yarn Needle, sewing needle, scissors, stitch markers.

Designer's Note
The same pattern is used for all three sizes.

BUNNY

HEAD

ROUND 1: (Right Side) Using Color A, make a **Magic Ring** (see Techniques), 6 sc in ring. DO NOT JOIN. (6 sc) Mark last stitch.

ROUND 2: 2 sc in each sc around. (12 sc) Move marker each round.

ROUND 3: [Sc in next sc, **inc** (see Special Stitches) in next sc] around. (18 sc)

ROUND 4: [Sc in each of next 2 sc, inc in next sc] around. (24 sc)

ROUND 5: [Sc in each of next 3 sc, inc in next sc] around. (30 sc)

ROUND 6: [Sc in each of next 4 sc, inc in next sc] around. (36 sc)

ROUND 7: [Sc in each of next 5 sc, inc in next sc] around. (42 sc)

ROUND 8: [Sc in each of next 6 sc, inc in next sc] around. (48 sc)

ROUNDS 9-17: Sc in each sc around. (48 sc)

ROUND 18: [Sc in each of next 6 sc, **sc-dec** (see Special Stitches)] around. (42 sc)

- Insert safety eyes between Rounds 16&17, with about 4 stitches between them.

- Start stuffing Head firmly, adding more as you go.

ROUND 19: [Sc in each of next 5 sc, sc-dec] around. (36 sc)

ROUND 20: [Sc in each of next 4 sc, sc-dec] around. (30 sc)

ROUND 21: [Sc in each of next 3 sc, sc-dec] around, **changing color** (see Techniques) to Color B in last st. (24 sc) Cut Color A and weave in ends. DO NOT FASTEN OFF COLOR B. Continue with Body.

BODY

ROUND 1: With Color B, [sc in each of next 3 sc, inc in next sc] around. (30 sc)

ROUNDS 2-3: Sc in each sc around. (30 sc)

ROUND 4: [Sc in each of next 4 sc, inc in next sc] around. (36 sc)

ROUNDS 5-7: Sc in each sc around. (36 sc)

ROUND 8: [Sc in each of next 5 sc, inc in next sc] around. (42 sc)

ROUNDS 9-11: Sc in each sc around. (42 sc)

ROUND 12: [Sc in each of next 6 sc, inc in next sc] around. (48 sc)

ROUNDS 13-15: Sc in each sc around. (48 sc)

ROUND 16: [Sc in each of next 7 sc, inc in next sc] around. (54 sc)

ROUNDS 17-22: Sc in each sc around. (54 sc)

ROUND 23: [Sc in each of next 7 sc, sc-dec] around. (48 sc)

- Start stuffing Body firmly, adding more as you go.

ROUND 24: [Sc in each of next 6 sc, sc-dec] around. (42 sc)

ROUND 25: [Sc in each of next 5 sc, sc-dec] around. (36 sc)

ROUND 26: [Sc in each of next 4 sc, sc-dec] around. (30 sc)

ROUND 27: [Sc in each of next 3 sc, sc-dec] around. (24 sc)

ROUND 28: [Sc in each of next 2 sc, sc-dec] around. (18 sc)

ROUND 29: [Sc in next sc, sc-dec] around. (12 sc)

ROUND 30: [Sc-dec] around. (6 sc) Fasten off leaving long tail for sewing.

- Finish stuffing Body.

- Using yarn needle and long tail, **close the opening** (see Techniques).

HAT

ROUNDS 1-8: Using Color B, repeat Rounds 1-8 of Head. At the end of Round 8, there are 48 sc.

ROUND 9: [Sc in each of next 15 sc, inc in next sc] 3 times. (51 sc)

ROUNDS 10-19: Sc in each sc around. (51 sc)
At the end of Round 19, change color to Color C (optional)

ROUND 20: Sc in each sc around. (51 sc)

ROUND 21: [Sc in each of next 15 sc, sc-dec] 3 times. (48 sc) Fasten off with **Invisible Join** (see Techniques) and weave in all ends.

- Position Hat on Head.
- Apply Blusher to Cheeks.

EARS (Make 2)

ROUNDS 1-2: Using Color B, repeat Rounds 1-2 of Head. At the end of Round 2, there are 12 sc.

ROUNDS 3-13: Sc in each sc around. (12 sc)

At the end of Round 13, Fasten off leaving long tail for sewing. Do not stuff Ears.

- Position the Ears on Hat, and using long tail and yarn needle, sew in place.

ARMS (Make 2)

ROUNDS 1-2: Using Color B, repeat Rounds 1-2 of Head. At the end of Round 2, there are 12 sc.

ROUND 3: [Sc in each of next 3 sc, inc in next sc] 3 times. (15 sc)

ROUNDS 4-9: Sc in each sc around. (15 sc)

At the end of Round 9, Fasten off leaving long tail for sewing.

- Stuff Arms firmly.
- Position the Arms on either side of the Body, and using long tail and yarn needle, sew in place.

TAIL

ROUNDS 1-3: Using Color A, repeat Rounds 1-3 of Arms. At the end of Round 3, there are 15 sc.

ROUND 4: Sc in each sc around. (15 sc)

ROUND 5: [Sc in each of next 3 sc, sc-dec] 3 times. (12 sc) Fasten off leaving long tail for sewing.

- Stuff Tail firmly.
- Position the Tail at center back of the Body, and using long tail and yarn needle, sew in place.

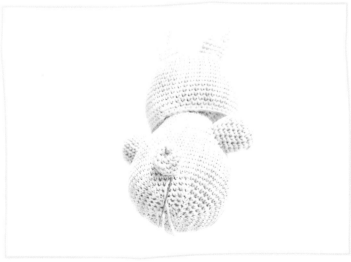

Reindeer

By Kristi Tullus

MATERIALS NEEDED

DMC Natura Just Cotton
Color A - Canelle (N37)
Color B - Tropic Brown (N22)
Color C - Nacar (N35)

Hook

Size C-2 (2.75 mm) or size suitable for yarn used.

Other

Polyester Fiberfill for stuffing
½" (12mm) Safety Eyes - 2
¾" (20mm) Doll Joints - 2 (optional) for Legs
⅝" (16 mm) Doll Joints - 2 (optional) for Arms
Dark Brown Embroidery Floss - for Nose
Length of Ribbon (optional) - for female Deer
Yarn Needle, sewing needle, scissors, stitch markers.

Designer's Tip
I prefer using the plastic doll joints. They
are easy to install as well as being durable
and washable.

DEER

HEAD

ROUND 1: (Right Side) Using Color A, make a **Magic Ring** (see Techniques), 6 sc in ring. DO NOT JOIN. (6 sc) Mark last stitch.

ROUND 2: 2 sc in each sc around. (12 sc) Move marker each round.

ROUND 3: [Sc in next sc, **inc** (see Special Stitches) in next sc] around. (18 sc)

ROUND 4: [Inc in next sc, sc in each of next 2 sc] around. (24 sc)

ROUND 5: [Sc in each of next 7 sc, inc in next sc] 3 times. (27 sc)

ROUND 6: Sc in each sc around. (27 sc)

ROUND 7: Sc in each of next 3 sc, inc in next sc, [sc in each of next 8 sc, inc in next sc] twice, sc in each of next 5 sc. (30 sc)

ROUND 8: Sc in each sc around. (30 sc)

ROUND 9: [Sc in each of next 9 sc, inc in next sc] 3 times. (33 sc)

ROUND 10: Sc in each sc around. (33 sc)

ROUND 11: Sc in each of next 4 sc, inc in next sc, [sc in each of next 10 sc, inc in next sc] twice, sc in each of next 6 sc. (36 sc)

ROUND 12: Sc in each of next 2 sc, inc in next sc, [sc in each of next 5 sc, inc in next sc] 5 times, sc in each of next 3 sc. (42 sc)

- Place a marker in the 22nd stitch on Round 12 – to mark center of the face.

ROUND 13: [Sc in each of next 6 sc, inc in next sc] around. (48 sc)

ROUND 14: Sc in each of next 19 sc, inc in next sc, sc in each of next 7 sc, inc in next sc, sc in each of next 20 sc. (50 sc)

ROUND 15: Sc in each of next 21 sc, inc in next sc, sc in each of next 5 sc, inc in next sc, sc in each of next 22 sc. (52 sc)

ROUND 16: [Sc in each of next 25 sc, inc in next sc] twice. (54 sc)

ROUND 17: Sc in each of next 23 sc, inc in next sc, sc in each of next 4 sc, inc in next sc, sc in each of next 25 sc. (56 sc) DO NOT FASTEN OFF.

- Insert Safety Eyes between Rounds 12 & 13, with 14 stitches (count 13 holes) between them.

- Add a bit of stuffing to the Muzzle and using Floss, embroider the Nose:

Insert the needle from inside the Head bringing it out just above the first round.

Make a few stitches to outline the shape and size of the nose.

Keeping even tension, make more stitches until all the gaps are filled.

Make a long stitch across the top of the nose to hide imperfections

Insert needle back into the Head and knot the two yarn tails together inside the Head.

ROUNDS 18-25: Sc in each sc around. (56 sc)

ROUND 26: Sc in each of next 5 sc, **sc-dec** (see Special Stitches), [sc in each of next 12 sc, sc-dec] 3 times, sc in each of next 7 sc. (52 sc)

ROUND 27: [Sc in each of next 11 sc, sc-dec] 4 times. (48 sc)

ROUND 28: Sc in each of next 4 sc, sc-dec, [sc in each of next 10 sc, sc-dec] 3 times, sc in each of next 6 sc. (44 sc)

- Start stuffing the Head firmly, adding more as you go.

ROUND 29: [Sc in each of next 9 sc, sc-dec] 4 times. (40 sc)

ROUND 30: Sc in each of next 3 sc, sc-dec, [sc in each of next 8 sc, sc-dec] 3 times, sc in each of next 5 sc. (36 sc)

ROUND 31: [Sc in each of next 7 sc, sc-dec] 4 times. (32 sc)

ROUND 32: Sc in each of next 2 sc, sc-dec, [sc in each of next 6 sc, sc-dec] 3 times, sc in each of next 4 sc. (28 sc)

ROUND 33: [Sc in each of next 5 sc, sc-dec] 4 times. (24 sc)

ROUND 34: [Sc-dec, sc in each of next 2 sc] 6 times. (18 sc)

ROUND 35: [Sc in next sc, sc-dec] 6 times. (12 sc)

ROUND 36: [Sc-dec] 6 times. (6 sc) **Fasten off** (see Techniques) leaving long tail.

- Finish stuffing the Head firmly.
- Using long tail and yarn needle, **close the opening** (see Techniques).
- Using Color A and yarn needle, shape the Head as follows:

Leaving a tail, insert the needle from the bottom of the Head (between Rounds 16 & 18), and bring it out right next to the eye.

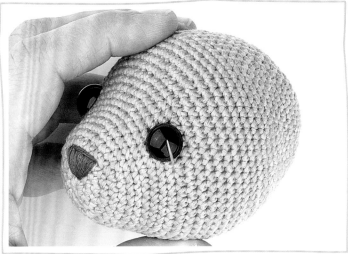

Then, about half way around the eye, insert the needle next to the eye and bring it out at the bottom of the Head (near the starting tail).

Gently tug the yarn tails, pulling the eye slightly into the Head.

Knot the yarn tails together. Weave in all ends. Repeat the shaping on the other eye.

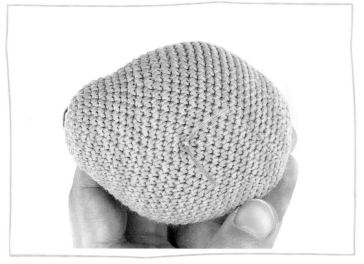

EARS (Make 2)

ROUND 1: (Right Side) Using Color A, make a Magic Ring, 6 sc in ring. DO NOT JOIN. (6 sc) Mark last stitch.

ROUND 2: [Inc in next sc, sc in next sc] 3 times. (9 sc) Move marker each round.

ROUND 3: [Sc in each of next 2 sc, inc in next sc] around. (12 sc)

ROUND 4: Sc in next sc, inc in next sc, [sc in each of next 3 sc, inc in next sc] twice, sc in each of next 2 sc. (15 sc)

ROUND 5: [Sc in each of next 4 sc, inc in next sc] around. (18 sc)

ROUND 6: Sc in each of next 2 sc, inc in next sc, [sc in each of next 5 sc, inc in next sc] twice, sc in each of next 3 sc. (21 sc)

ROUND 7: [Sc in each of next 6 sc, inc in next sc] around. (24 sc)

ROUND 8: [Sc in each of next 11 sc, inc in next sc] twice. (26 sc)

ROUND 9: Sc in each of next 5 sc, inc in next sc, sc in each of next 12 sc, inc in next sc, sc in each of next 7 sc. (28 sc)

ROUNDS 10-15: Sc in each sc around. (28 sc)

ROUND 16: [Sc-dec, sc in each of next 12 sc] twice. (26 sc)

ROUND 17: [Sc-dec, sc in each of next 11 sc] twice. (24 sc)

ROUND 18: [Sc-dec, sc in each of next 4 sc] 4 times. (20 sc) Fasten off leaving long tail for sewing. (Do not stuff the Ears)

Using long tail and yarn needle, position the Ears just behind Round 21 of the Head, leaving 21-22 stitches between them.

Flatten the Ear and start sewing it to the Head.

When you reach the center, fold the Ear in half...

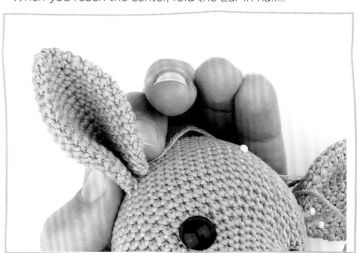

And sew the second side right next to the first.

ANTLERS (Optional) - Make 2 for male Deer

Note Make the three Tines first, and then join as you go.

Tine 1

ROUND 1: (Right Side) Using Color C, make a Magic Ring, 6 sc in ring. DO NOT JOIN. (6 sc) Mark last stitch.

ROUNDS 2-4: Sc in each sc around. (6 sc) Move marker each round.

ROUND 5: Sc in each of next 3 sc, inc in next sc, sc in each of next 2 sc. (7 sc)

ROUND 6: Sc in each sc around. (7 sc)

ROUND 7: Sc in each of next 4 sc, inc in next sc, sc in each of next 2 sc. (8 sc)

ROUND 8: Sc in each sc around. (8 sc)

ROUND 9: Sc in each of next 4 sc. Leave remaining sts unworked. Sl st in next stitch and Fasten off. Mark the stitch after the sl st. Do not close opening. Weave in ends.

- Stuff the Tine firmly and set aside.

Tine 2

ROUNDS 1-3: Repeat Rounds 1-3 of Tine 1. (6 sc)

ROUND 4: Sc in each of next 3 sc, inc in next sc, sc in each of next 2 sc. (7 sc)

ROUND 5: Sc in each sc around. (7 sc)

ROUND 6: Sc in each of next 4 sc, inc in next sc, sc in each of next 2 sc. (8 sc)

ROUNDS 7-8: Sc in each sc around. (8 sc)

ROUND 9: Sc in each of next 4 sc. Leave remaining sts unworked. Sl st in next stitch and Fasten off. Mark the stitch after the sl st. Do not close opening. Weave in ends.

- Stuff the Tine firmly and set aside.

Tine 3

ROUNDS 1-4: Repeat Rounds 1-4 of Tine 2.

ROUNDS 5-6: Sc in each sc around. (7 sc) DO NOT FASTEN OFF.

- Stuff the Tine firmly.

ROUND 7 (first joining round): Sc in next sc (on Tine 3), working on Tine 2, starting in marked st, sc in each of next 8 sc, working back on Tine 3, sc in each of next 2 sc, sc-dec, sc in each of next 2 sc. (14 sc)

ROUND 8: Sc-dec, sc in each of next 6 sc, sc-dec, sc in each of next 4 sc. (12 sc)

ROUND 9: [Sc-dec, sc in each of next 4 sc] twice. (10 sc)

ROUND 10: Sc in each sc around. (10 sc) DO NOT FASTEN OFF.

- Start stuffing the Antler firmly, adding more as you go.

ROUND 11: Sc in each of next 7 sc, sc-dec, sc in next sc. (9 sc)

ROUNDS 12-13: Sc in each sc around. (9 sc)

ROUND 14 (second joining round): Sc in each of next 4 sc (on Antler), working on Tine 1, starting in marked st, sc in each of next 8 sc, working back on Antler, sc in each of next 5 sc. (17 sc)

ROUND 15: Sc in each of next 3 sc, sc-dec, sc in each of next 6 sc, sc-dec, sc in each of next 4 sc. (15 sc)

ROUND 16: Sc in next sc, [sc-dec] twice, sc in each of next 3 sc, [sc-dec] twice, sc in each of next 3 sc. (11 sc)

ROUNDS 17-18: Sc in each sc around. (11 sc)

ROUND 19: Sc-dec, sc in each of next 9 sc. (10 sc)

ROUNDS 20-24: Sc in each sc around. (10 sc)

At the end of Round 24, fasten off leaving long tail for sewing.

- Stuff the Antler firmly.

- Repeat for second Antler.

Using long tail and yarn needle, position the Antlers just behind Round 21 on Head, leaving about 10-11 stitches between them, and sew in place.

ARMS (Make 2)

ROUNDS 1-4: Using Color B, repeat Rounds 1-4 of Head. At the end of Round 4, there are 24 sc.

ROUND 5: Working in **back loops** only (see Techniques), sc in each sc around. (24 sc)

ROUND 6: Working in both loops, sc in each of next 7 sc, sc-dec, [sc in each of next 2 sc, sc-dec] twice, sc in each of next 7 sc. (21 sc)

ROUND 7: Sc in each of next 8 sc, sc-dec, sc in next sc, sc-dec, sc in each of next 8 sc. (19 sc)

ROUND 8: [Sc in each of next 5 sc, sc-dec] twice, sc in each of next 5 sc. (17 sc)

ROUND 9: Sc-dec, sc in each of next 6 sc, sc-dec, sc in each of next 7 sc, **change color** (see Techniques) to Color A in last st. (15 sc) DO NOT FASTEN OFF.

- Stuff the Hoof firmly.

Using a separate strand of Color B and yarn needle, insert the needle from the top, leaving a short yarn tail, and bring it out between the last two rounds.

Then, going straight down, insert the needle just above the first round.

Bring the needle out through the opening, near where the yarn tail is.

Using the yarn tails, pull the stitch tight and knot the ends together.

- Start stuffing the Arm firmly, adding more as you go.

ROUND 10: With Color A, sc in each of next 7 sc, sc-dec, sc in each of next 6 sc. (14 sc)

ROUND 11: Sc in each sc around. (14 sc)

ROUND 12: Sc in each of next 7 sc, sc-dec, sc in each of next 5 sc. (13 sc)

ROUNDS 13-14: Sc in each sc around. (13 sc)

ROUND 15: Sc in each of next 7 sc, sc-dec, sc in each of next 4 sc. (12 sc)

ROUNDS 16-17: Sc in each sc around. (12 sc)

ROUND 18: Sc in each of next 7 sc, sc-dec, sc in each of next 3 sc. (11 sc)

ROUNDS 19-30: Sc in each sc around. (11 sc)

For Left Arm only: Sc in each of next 6 sc. Move marker to last st. This is now the last st of the round from now on.

For Both Arms:

- Insert the arm joint (optional) – (see Jointed Toys) between Rounds 29 & 30, positioning it so that the stem faces outwards and straight towards Body.

ROUND 31: [Sc-dec] 5 times. Leave remaining st unworked. Fasten off leaving long tail for sewing.

- Finish stuffing the Arm firmly.

- Using long tail and yarn needle, close the opening and weave in ends.

LEGS (Make 2)

ROUNDS 1-4: Using Color B, repeat Rounds 1-4 of Head. At the end of Round 4, there are 24 sc.

ROUND 5: [Sc in each of next 3 sc, inc in next sc] around. (30 sc)

ROUND 6: Working in **back loops** only, sc in each sc around. (30 sc)

ROUND 7: Working in both loops, sc in each of next 8 sc, sc-dec, [sc in each of next 2 sc, sc-dec] 3 times, sc in each of next 8 sc. (26 sc)

ROUND 8: Sc in each of next 9 sc, sc-dec, [sc in next sc, sc-dec] twice, sc in each of next 9 sc. (23 sc)

ROUND 9: Sc in each of next 5 sc, sc-dec. sc in each of next 9 sc, sc-dec, sc in each of next 5 sc. (21 sc)

ROUND 10: Sc-dec, sc in each of next 8 sc, sc-dec, sc in each of next 9 sc, changing to Color A in last st. (19 sc) DO NOT FASTEN OFF.

- Stuff the Hoof firmly.

- Following the Arm instructions, make the long vertical stitch along the front of the Hoof and draw it tight.

- Start stuffing the Leg firmly, adding more as you go.

ROUND 11: With Color A, sc in each of next 6 sc, sc-dec, sc in each of next 3 sc, sc-dec, sc in each of next 6 sc. (17 sc)

ROUND 12: Sc in each of next 8 sc, sc dec, sc in each of next 7 sc. (16 sc)

ROUND 13: Sc in each sc around. (16 sc)

ROUND 14: Sc in each of next 8 sc, sc-dec, sc in each of next 6 sc. (15 sc)

ROUNDS 15-16: Sc in each sc around. (15 sc)

ROUND 17: Sc in each of next 8 sc, sc-dec, sc in each of next 5 sc. (14 sc)

ROUNDS 18-32: Sc in each sc around. (14 sc)

For Left Leg only: Sc in each of next 7 sc. Move marker to last st. This is now the last st of the round from now on.

For Both Legs:

- Insert the leg joint (optional) between Rounds 31 & 32, positioning it so that the stem faces outwards and straight towards Body.

ROUND 33: Sc in each of next 2 sc, sc-dec, sc in each of next 7 sc, sc-dec, sc in next sc. (12 sc)

ROUND 34: [Sc-dec] 6 times. Fasten off leaving long tail for sewing.

- Finish stuffing the Leg firmly.

- Using long tail and yarn needle, close the opening and weave in ends..

BODY

ROUNDS 1-4: Using Color A, repeat Rounds 1-4 of Head. At the end of Round 4, there are 24 sc.

ROUND 5: [Sc in each of next 3 sc, inc in next sc] around. (30 sc)

ROUND 6: Sc in next sc, inc in next sc, [sc in each of next 4 sc, inc in next sc] 5 times, sc in each of next 3 sc. (36 sc)

ROUND 7: Sc in each of next 3 sc, inc in next sc, [sc in each of next 8 sc, inc in next sc] 3 times, sc in each of next 5 sc. (40 sc)

ROUND 8: [Sc in each of next 9 sc, inc in next sc] around. (44 sc)

ROUNDS 9-16: Sc in each sc around. (44 sc)

- Using the last marked stitch as center back of the Body, attach the Legs to either side of the Body (see Jointed Toys), between Rounds 9 & 10.

ROUND 17: [Sc in each of next 9 sc, sc-dec] 4 times. (40 sc)

ROUND 18: Sc in each of next 3 sc, sc-dec, [sc in each of next 8 sc, sc-dec] 3 times, sc in each of next 5 sc. (36 sc)

ROUND 19: [Sc in each of next 7 sc, sc-dec] 4 times. (32 sc)

ROUND 20: Sc in each sc around. (32 sc)

ROUND 21: [Sc-dec, sc in each of next 14 sc] twice. (30 sc)

- Start stuffing the Body firmly, adding more as you go.

ROUND 22: Sc in each sc around. (30 sc)

ROUND 23: Sc in each of next 12 sc, sc-dec, sc in each of next 4 sc, sc-dec, sc in each of next 10 sc. (28 sc)

ROUND 24: Sc in each sc around. (28 sc)

ROUND 25: [Sc-dec, sc in each of next 5 sc] 4 times. (24 sc)

ROUND 26: Sc in each sc around. (24 sc)

ROUND 27: Sc in each of next 9 sc, sc-dec, sc in each of next 4 sc, sc-dec, sc in each of next 7 sc. (22 sc)

ROUND 28: Sc in each sc around. (22 sc)

ROUND 29: Sc in each of next 5 sc, sc-dec, sc in each of next 9 sc, sc-dec, sc in each of next 4 sc. (20 sc)

ROUNDS 30-33: Sc in each sc around. (20 sc)

ROW 34: Sc in each of next 5 sc. Leave rem sts unworked. Fasten off leaving long tail for sewing.

- Attach the Arms to either side of the Body, between Rounds 29 & 30.

TAIL

ROUND 1: (Right Side) Using Color A, make a Magic Ring, 6 sc in ring. DO NOT JOIN. (6 sc) Mark last stitch.

ROUND 2: [Sc in each of next 2 sc, inc in next sc] twice. (8 sc) Move marker each round.

ROUND 3: Sc in next sc, inc in next sc, sc in each of next 3 sc, inc in next sc, sc in each of next 2 sc. (10 sc)

ROUND 4: Sc in each sc around. (10 sc)

ROUND 5: [Sc-dec, sc in each of next 3 sc] twice. (8 sc) Fasten off leaving long tail for sewing. Do not stuff the Tail.

Flatten the Tail and position it at the 8th round at center

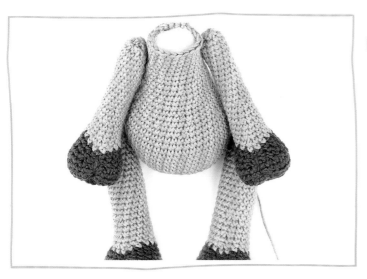

back of Body. Using long tail and yarn needle, sew in place.

- Finish stuffing the Body firmly.

- Using long tail and yarn needle, position and sew the Body to the Head, adding a bit more stuffing before closing. (The front edge of the Body is just behind Round 15 of Head.)

Red Fox

By Kristi Tullus

FINISHED SIZE
About 11" (28 cm) tall.

MATERIALS NEEDED

DMC Natura Medium Just Cotton
Color A - Red (#05)
Color B - Taupe (#11)
Color C - Natural (#03)

Hook
Size G-6 (4.00 mm) or size suitable for yarn used.

Other
Polyester Fiberfill for stuffing
⅜" (10 mm) Safety Eyes - 2
½" (12 mm) Safety Nose - 1
¾" (20 mm) Doll Joints - 2 (optional) for Legs
⅝" (16 mm) Doll Joints - 2 (optional) for Arms
Yarn Needle, sewing needle, scissors, stitch markers.

Designer's Tip
I prefer using the plastic doll joints. They are easy to install as well as being durable and washable.

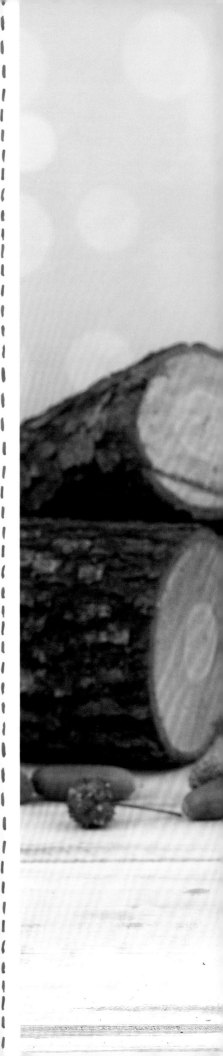

RED FOX

HEAD

ROUND 1: (Right Side) Using Color C, make a **Magic Ring** (see Techniques), 6 sc in ring. DO NOT JOIN. (6 sc) Mark last stitch.

ROUND 2: 2 sc in each sc around. (12 sc) Move marker each round.

ROUND 3: [Sc in each of next 3 sc, **inc** (see Special Stitches) in next sc] around. (15 sc)

ROUND 4: Sc in each sc around. (15 sc)

ROUND 5: [Inc in next sc, sc in each of next 2 sc] around. (20 sc)

ROUND 6: Sc in each sc around. (20 sc)

ROUND 7: [Sc in each of next 3 sc, inc in next sc] around, **changing color** (see Techniques) to Color A in last st. (25 sc) Cut Color C and weave in ends.

ROUND 8: Using Color A, sc in each sc around. (25 sc)

ROUND 9: [Inc in next sc, sc in next sc] 3 times, hdc in next sc, [2 hdc in next sc] 8 times, hdc in next sc, [sc in next sc, inc in next sc] 4 times, sc in next sc. (40 sts)

ROUND 10: Sc in each of next 11 sts, hdc in next st, [2 hdc in next st, hdc in next st] 7 times, sc in each of next 14 sts. (47 sts)

ROUND 11: Sc in each of next 8 sts, inc in next st, [sc in each of next 6 sts, inc in next st] 4 times, sc in each of next 10 sts. (52 sts)

ROUND 12: Sc in each of next 22 sc, inc in next sc, sc in each of next 5 sc, inc in next sc, sc in each of next 23 sc. (54 sc)

ROUND 13: Sc in next sc, inc in next sc, sc in each of next 49 sc, inc in next sc, sc in each of next 2 sc. (56 sc)

- Insert Safety Eyes between Rounds 9 & 10, with 13 stitches (count 12 holes) between them.

- Insert Safety Nose between Rounds 1 & 2.

ROUNDS 14-21: Sc in each sc around. (56 sc)

ROUND 22: Sc in each of next 5 sc, **sc-dec** (see Special Stitches), [sc in each of next 12 sc, sc-dec] 3 times, sc in each of next 7 sc. (52 sc)

ROUND 23: [Sc in each of next 11 sc, sc-dec] 4 times. (48 sc)

ROUND 24: Sc in each of next 4 sc, sc-dec, [sc in each of next 10 sc, sc-dec] 3 times, sc in each of next 6 sc. (44 sc)

ROUND 25: [Sc in each of next 9 sc, sc-dec] 4 times. (40 sc)

ROUND 26: Sc in each of next 3 sc, sc-dec, [sc in each of next 8 sc, sc-dec] 3 times, sc in each of next 5 sc. (36 sc)

- Start stuffing the Head firmly, adding more as you go.

ROUND 27: [Sc in each of next 7 sc, sc-dec] 4 times. (32 sc)

ROUND 28: Sc in each of next 2 sc, sc-dec, [sc in each of next 6 sc, sc-dec] 3 times, sc in each of next 4 sc. (28 sc)

ROUND 29: [Sc in each of next 5 sc, sc-dec] 4 times. (24 sc)

ROUND 30: [Sc-dec, sc in each of next 2 sc] 6 times. (18 sc)

ROUND 31: [Sc in next sc, sc-dec] 6 times. (12 sc)

ROUND 32: [Sc-dec] 6 times. (6 sc) **Fasten off** (see Techniques) leaving long tail.

- Finish stuffing the Head firmly.

- Using long tail and yarn needle, **close the opening** (see Techniques) and weave in ends.

- Using Color A and yarn needle, shape the Head as follows:

Leaving a tail, insert the needle from the bottom of the Head (between Rounds 15 & 18), and bring it out right next to the eye.

Then, about half way around the eye, insert the needle next to the eye and bring it out at the bottom of the Head (near the starting tail).

Gently tug the yarn tails, pulling the eye slightly into the Head.

Knot the yarn tails together. Weave in all ends. Repeat the shaping on the other eye.

INNER EARS (Make 2)

ROUND 1: (Right Side) Using Color C, make a Magic Ring, 6 sc in ring. DO NOT JOIN. (6 sc) Mark last stitch.

ROUND 2: [Sc in next sc, **inc3** (see Special Stitches) in next sc] around. (12 sc) Move marker each round.

ROUND 3: Sc in each of next 2 sc, inc3 (in center sc of 3-sc group), [sc in each of next 3 sc, inc3 in next sc] twice, sc in next sc. (18 sc)

ROUND 4: Sc in each of next 3 sc, inc3 (in center sc of 3-sc group), [sc in each of next 5 sc, inc3 in next sc] twice, sc in each of next 2 sc. (24 sc) Fasten off and weave in all ends.

OUTER EARS (Make 2)

ROUNDS 1-3: Using Color A, repeat Round 1-3 of Inner Ears.

ROUND 4: Sc in each of next 3 sc, inc3 (insert Marker in center sc of 3-sc group), [sc in each of next 5 sc, inc3 in next sc] twice, sc in each of next 2 sc. (24 sc) Fasten off and weave in all ends.

- With right sides facing (wrong sides together), hold an Inner and Outer Ear together, matching shaping and with Inner Ear facing.

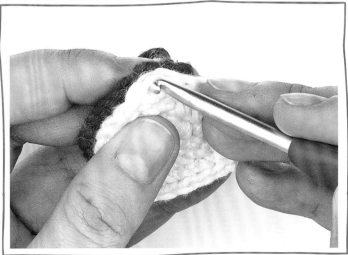

JOINING ROW: Using Color A, leaving short tail, working through both thicknesses, join with sl st to marked st (center sc of 3-sc group), sc in same st as joining, sc in each of next 6 sts, change to Color B, with Color B, sc in next st, inc-3 in next st (center sc of 3-sc group), sc in next sc, change to Color A, with Color A, sc in each of next 7 sts, sl st in same st as last sc. Leave remaining sts unworked. Fasten off leaving long tail for sewing.

Designer's Tip: When you change colors, do not tie the yarn tails together. At the end of the Joining Row, pull all the tails to the wrong side and knot them together inside the Ear.

LEFT ARM

ROUND 1: (Right Side) Using Color B, make a Magic Ring, 6 sc in ring. DO NOT JOIN. (6 sc) Mark last stitch.

ROUND 2: *[Inc3 in next sc] twice, sc in next sc; rep from * once more. (14 sc)

ROUNDS 3-5: Sc in each sc around. (14 sc)

ROUND 6: Sc in each of next 3 sc, inc in next sc, sc in each of next 5 sc, [sc-dec] twice, sc in next sc. (13 sc)

ROUND 7: Sc in each of next 4 sc, inc in next sc, sc in each of next 5 sc, sc-dec, sc in next sc. (13 sc)

ROUND 8: Sc in each of next 10 sc, sc-dec, sc in next sc. (12 sc)

- Start stuffing the Hands firmly, adding more to the Arms as you go.

ROUND 9: Sc in each of next 10 sc, sc-dec. (11 sc)

ROUND 10: Sc in each of next 9 sc, sc-dec. (10 sc)

ROUND 11: Sc in each sc around, changing to Color A in last st. (10) Cut Color B and weave in ends.

ROUNDS 12-23: Using Color A, sc in each sc around. (10 sc)

- Insert the arm joint (optional) (see Jointed Toys) between Rounds 20 & 21, positioning it so that the stem faces outwards and straight towards Body.

ROUND 24: [Sc-dec] 5 times. (5 sc) Fasten off leaving long tail for sewing.

- Finish stuffing the Arm firmly.

- Using long tail and yarn needle, close the opening.

RIGHT ARM

ROUNDS 1-5: Repeat Rounds 1-5 of Left Arm.

ROUND 6: Sc in each of next 2 sc, [sc-dec] twice, sc in each of next 5 sc, inc in next sc, sc in each of next 2 sc. (13 sc)

ROUND 7: Sc in each of next 2 sc, sc-dec, sc in each of next 5 sc, inc in next sc, sc in each of next 3 sc. (13 sc)

ROUND 8: Sc in each of next 2 sc, sc-dec, sc in each of next 9 sc. (12 sc)

- Start stuffing the Hands firmly, adding more to the Arms as you go.

ROUND 9: Sc in next sc, sc-dec, sc in each of next 9 sc. (11 sc)

ROUND 10: Sc in next sc, sc-dec, sc in each of next 8 sc. (10 sc)

ROUNDS 11-22: Repeat Rounds 11-22 of Left Arm.

ROUND 23: Sc in each of next 6 sc, [sc-dec] twice. (8 sc)

- Insert the arm joint (optional) between Rounds 20 & 21, positioning it so that the stem faces outwards and straight towards Body.

ROUND 24: [Sc-dec] 3 times. Leave remaining sts unworked. Fasten off leaving long tail for sewing.

- Finish stuffing the Arm firmly.

- Using long tail and yarn needle, close the opening.

LEGS (Make 2)

ROUND 1: (Right Side) Using Color B, make a Magic Ring, 6 sc in ring. DO NOT JOIN. (6 sc) Mark last stitch.

ROUND 2: 2 sc in each sc around. (12 sc) Move marker each round.

ROUND 3: [Sc in next sc, inc in next sc] around. (18 sc)

ROUND 4: [Sc in each of next 3 sc, inc in next sc, sc in each of next 4 sc, inc in next sc] twice. (22 sc)

ROUND 5: Sc in each sc around. (22 sc)

ROUND 6: Sc in each of next 7 sc, sc-dec, sc in each of next 2 sc, sc-dec, sc in each of next 9 sc. (20 sc)

ROUND 7: Sc in each of next 5 sc, sc-dec, [sc in next sc, sc-dec] twice, sc in each of next 7 sc. (17 sc)

ROUND 8: Sc in each of next 5 sc, sc-dec, sc in each of next 2 sc, sc-dec, sc in each of next 6 sc. (15 sc)

ROUND 9: Sc in each of next 6 sc, sc-dec, sc in each of next 7 sc. (14 sc)

- Start stuffing the Feet firmly, adding more to the Legs as you go.

ROUND 10: Sc in each sc around. (14 sc)

ROUND 11: Sc in each of next 6 sc, sc-dec, sc in each of next 6 sc. (13 sc)

ROUNDS 12-16: Sc in each sc around, changing to Color A in last st. (13) Cut Color B and weave in ends.

ROUNDS 17-26: Using Color A, sc in each sc around. (13 sc)

For Left Leg only: Sc in each of next 6 sc. Move marker to last st. This is now the last st of the round from now on.

For Both Legs:

- Insert the leg joint (optional) between Rounds 25 & 26, positioning it so that the stem faces outwards and straight towards Body.

ROUND 27: Sc-dec, sc in each of next 6 sc, sc-dec, sc in each of next 3 sc. (11 sc)

ROUND 28: [Sc in next sc, sc-dec] 5 times. Leave remaining st unworked. Fasten off leaving long tail for sewing.

- Finish stuffing the Leg firmly.

- Using long tail and yarn needle, close the opening.

BODY

ROUND 1: (Right Side) Using Color A, make a Magic Ring, 6 sc in ring. DO NOT JOIN. (6 sc) Mark last stitch.

ROUND 2: 2 sc in each sc around. (12 sc) Move marker each round.

ROUND 3: [Sc in next sc, inc in next sc] around. (18 sc)

ROUND 4: [Inc in next sc, sc in each of next 2 sc] around. (24 sc)

ROUND 5: [Sc in each of next 3 sc, inc in next sc] around. (30 sc)

ROUND 6: Sc in next sc, inc in next sc, [sc in each of next 4 sc, inc in next sc] 5 times, sc in each of next 3 sc. (36 sc)

ROUND 7: Sc in each of next 3 sc, inc in next sc, [sc in each of next 8 sc, inc in next sc] 3 times, sc in each of next 5 sc. (40 sc)

ROUND 8: [Sc in each of next 9 sc, inc in next sc] around. (44 sc)

ROUNDS 9-16: Sc in each sc around (44 sc) DO NOT FASTEN OFF.

- Using the last marked stitch as center back of the Body, attach the Legs to either side of the Body (see Jointed Toys), between Rounds 9 & 10.

ROUND 17: [Sc in each of next 9 sc, sc-dec] 4 times. (40 sc)

ROUND 18: Sc in each of next 3 sc, sc-dec, [sc in each of next 8 sc, sc-dec] 3 times, sc in each of next 5 sc. (36 sc)

ROUND 19: [Sc in each of next 7 sc, sc-dec] 4 times. (32 sc)

ROUND 20: Sc in each sc around. (32 sc)

ROUND 21: [Sc-dec, sc in each of next 14 sc] twice. (30 sc)

- Start stuffing the Body firmly, adding more as you go.

ROUND 22: Sc in each sc around. (30 sc)

ROUND 23: Sc in each of next 12 sc, sc-dec, sc in each of next 4 sc, sc-dec, sc in each of next 10 sc. (28 sc)

ROUND 24: Sc in each sc around. (28 sc)

ROUND 25: [Sc-dec, sc in each of next 5 sc] 4 times. (24 sc)

ROUND 26: Sc in each sc around. (24 sc)

ROUND 27: Sc in each of next 9 sc, sc-dec, sc in each of next 4 sc, sc-dec, sc in each of next 7 sc. (22 sc)

ROUND 28: Sc in each sc around. (22 sc)

ROUND 29: Sc in each of next 5 sc, sc-dec, sc in each of next 9 sc, sc-dec, sc in each of next 4 sc. (20 sc)

ROUNDS 30-31: Sc in each sc around. (20 sc)

ROW 32: Sc in each of next 5 sc. Leave rem sts unworked. Fasten off leaving long tail for sewing.

- Attach the Arms to either side of the Body, between Rounds 27 & 28.

Finish stuffing the Body firmly.

- Using long tail and yarn needle, position and sew the Body to the Head, adding a bit more stuffing before closing. (The front edge of the Body is just behind Round 13 of Head.)

TAIL

ROUND 1: (Right Side) Using Color C, make a Magic Ring, 6 sc in ring. DO NOT JOIN. (6 sc) Mark last stitch.

ROUND 2: [Sc in next sc, inc in next sc] 3 times. (9 sc) Move marker each round.

ROUND 3: [Inc in next sc, sc in each of next 2 sc] 3 times. (12 sc)

ROUND 4: [Sc in each of next 2 sc, inc in next sc] 4 times. (16 sc)

ROUND 5: Sc in next sc, inc in next sc, [sc in each of next 3 sc, inc in next sc] 3 times, sc in each of next 2 sc, changing to Color A in last st. (20 sc)

ROUNDS 6-9: Using Color A, sc in each sc around. (20 sc)

ROUND 10: [Sc-dec, sc in each of next 8 sc] twice. (18 sc)

- Start stuffing the Tail firmly, adding more as you go.

ROUND 11: Sc in each sc around. (18 sc)

ROUND 12: Sc in each of next 4 sc, sc-dec, sc in each of next 8 sc, sc-dec, sc in each of next 3 sc. (16 sc)

ROUND 13: Sc in each sc around. (16 sc)

ROUND 14: Sc in each of next 7 sc, sc-dec, sc in each of next 7 sc. (15 sc)

ROUND 15: Sc in each sc around. (15 sc)

ROUND 16: Sc in each of next 7 sc, sc-dec, sc in each of next 6 sc. (14 sc)

ROUNDS 17-18: Sc in each sc around. (14 sc)

ROUND 19: Sc in each of next 7 sc, sc-dec, sc in each of next 5 sc. (13 sc)

ROUNDS 20-21: Sc in each sc around. (13 sc)

ROUND 22: Sc in each of next 7 sc, sc-dec, sc in each of next 4 sc. (12 sc)

ROUNDS 23-24: Sc in each sc around. (12 sc)

ROUND 25: [Sc in next sc, sc-dec] 4 times. (8 sc) Fasten off leaving long tail for sewing.

- Finish stuffing the Tail firmly.

- Using long tail and yarn needle, position the Tail just above Round 8 of Body and sew in place.

Popsy The Doll

By Tine Nielsen

FINISHED SIZE
About 12" (30 cm) tall.

MATERIALS NEEDED

DMC Natura Just Cotton
Color A - Nacar (N35) for skin
Color B - Amaranto (N33) for Dress
Color C - Geranium (N52) for Skirt
Color D - Siena (N41) for Hair
Color E - Noir (N11) for Shoes

Hook
Size C-2 (2.75 mm) or size suitable for yarn used.

Other
Polyester Fiberfill for stuffing
¼" (6 mm) Safety Eyes - 2
Cosmetic Blusher (optional) for cheeks
Yarn Needle, sewing needle, scissors, stitch markers.

DOLL

HEAD

ROUND 1: (Right Side) Using Color A, make a **Magic Ring** (see Techniques), 6 sc in ring. DO NOT JOIN. (6 sc) Mark last stitch.

ROUND 2: 2 sc in each sc around. (12 sc) Move marker each round.

ROUND 3: [Sc in next sc, **inc** (see Special Stitches) in next sc] around. (18 sc)

ROUND 4: [Sc in each of next 2 sc, inc in next sc] around. (24 sc)

ROUND 5: [Sc in each of next 3 sc, inc in next sc] around. (30 sc)

ROUND 6: [Sc in each of next 4 sc, inc in next sc] around. (36 sc)

ROUND 7: [Sc in each of next 5 sc, inc in next sc] around. (42 sc)

ROUND 8: [Sc in each of next 6 sc, inc in next sc] around. (48 sc)

ROUND 9: [Sc in each of next 7 sc, inc in next sc] around. (54 sc)

ROUND 10: [Sc in each of next 8 sc, inc in next sc] around. (60 sc)

ROUND 11: [Sc in each of next 9 sc, inc in next sc] around. (66 sc)

ROUNDS 12-23: Sc in each sc around. (66 sc)

- Insert Safety Eyes between Rounds 15 & 16, with about 8 sts between them.

ROUND 24: [Sc in each of next 9 sc, sc-dec] around. (60 sc)

ROUND 25: [Sc in each of next 8 sc, sc-dec] around. (54 sc)

ROUND 26: [Sc in each of next 7 sc, sc-dec] around. (48 sc)

ROUND 27: [Sc in each of next 6 sc, sc-dec] around. (42 sc)

ROUND 28: [Sc in each of next 5 sc, sc-dec] around. (36 sc)

ROUND 29: [Sc in each of next 4 sc, sc-dec] around. (30 sc)

- Start stuffing Head firmly, adding more as you go.

ROUND 30: [Sc in each of next 3 sc, sc-dec] around. (24 sc)

ROUNDS 31-32: Sc in each sc around. (24 sc)
At the end of Round 32, fasten off leaving long tail for sewing to Body.

HAIR

ROUNDS 1-23: Using Color D, repeat Rounds 1-23 of Head. At the end of Round 23, there are 66 sc.

ROUND 24: Sc in next sc, hdc in next sc, dc in each of next 5 sc, hdc in next sc, sc in each of next 43 sc, hdc in next sc, dc in each of next 12 sc, hdc in next sc, sl st in next sc. (66 sts) Fasten off leaving long tail for sewing.

- Position Hair on Head, so that the doll has a 'side parting' and pin in place.

- Using long tail and yarn needle, sew Hair to Head.

Hair Buns (make 2)

ROUNDS 1-6: Using Color D, repeat Rounds 1-6 of Head. At the end of Round 6, there are 36 sc.

ROUNDS 7-11: Sc in each sc around. (36 sc)

ROUND 12: [Sc in each of next 4 sc, sc-dec] around. (30 sc)

ROUND 13: [Sc in each of next 3 sc, sc-dec] around. (24 sc) Fasten off leaving long tail for sewing.

- Stuff the Buns firmly and position them on either side of the Head, about at Round 20.

- Using long tail and yarn needle, sew them in place.

- Using a separate strand of Color D, wrap it around the bun and secure at the back. Repeat for other Bun.

- Using Color A and yarn needle, embroider a Nose between Rounds 17 & 18, by making 4 to 5 horizontal stitches.

- Apply a little Blusher to the Cheeks.

LEGS (make 2)

ROUNDS 1-6: Using Color A, repeat Rounds 1-6 of Head. At the end of Round 6, there are 36 sc.

ROUNDS 7-11: Sc in each sc around. (36 sc)

ROUND 12: Sc in each of next 14 sc, [**sc-dec** (see Special Stitches)] 4 times, sc in each of next 14 sc. (32 sc)

- Start stuffing Leg firmly, adding more as you go.

ROUND 13: Sc in each of next 10 sc, [sc in next sc, sc-dec] 4 times, sc in each of next 10 sc. (28 sc)

ROUND 14: Sc in each of next 6 sc, [sc in each of next 2 sc, sc-dec] 4 times, sc in each of next 6 sc. (24 sc)

ROUND 15: [Sc in each of next 2 sc, sc-dec] 6 times. (18 sc)

ROUNDS 16-36: Sc in each sc around. (18 sc)

For the first Leg, at the end of Round 36, fasten off.

For the second Leg, at the end of Round 36, sl st in next sc. DO NOT FASTEN OFF. Continue with Body.

BODY / DRESS

ROUND 1: Ch 3, working on first Leg, making sure both Feet are pointing the same way, and starting at the inner leg, sc in each of next 18 sts, sc in each of next 3 ch-sts, working on second Leg, sc in each of next 18 sts, working in unused lps on other side of ch-3, sc in each of next 3 ch. (42 sc)

ROUND 2: Sc in each sc around. (42 sc)

ROUND 3: [Sc in each of next 6 sc, inc in next sc] around. (48 sc)

ROUND 4: Sc in each sc around. (48 sc)

ROUND 5: [Sc in each of next 7 sc, inc in next sc] around. (54 sc)

ROUND 6: Sc in each sc around. (54 sc)

ROUND 7: [Sc in each of next 8 sc, inc in next sc] around. (60 sc)

ROUND 8: Sc in each sc around, **changing color** (see Techniques) to Color C in last st. (60 sc)

ROUND 9: With Color C, sc in each sc around. (60 sc)

ROUND 10: Working in **back loops** only (see Techniques), sc in each sc around, changing to Color B in last st. (60 sc)

ROUND 11: With Color B, working in both loops, sc in each sc around. (60 sc)

ROUND 12: Working in **back loops** only, sc in each sc around. (60 sc)

ROUND 13: Working in both loops, sc in each sc around. (60 sc)

ROUND 14: [Sc in each of next 8 sc, sc-dec] 6 times. (54 sc)

ROUNDS 15-16: Sc in each sc around. (54 sc)

ROUND 17: [Sc in each of next 7 sc, sc-dec] 6 times. (48 sc)

ROUNDS 18-19: Sc in each sc around. (48 sc)

ROUND 20: [Sc in each of next 6 sc, sc-dec] 6 times. (42 sc)

ROUND 21: Sc in each sc around. (42 sc)

- Start stuffing Body, adding more as you go.

ROUND 22: [Sc in each of next 5 sc, sc-dec] 6 times. (36 sc)

ROUND 23: Sc in each sc around. (36 sc)

ROUND 24: [Sc in each of next 4 sc, sc-dec] 6 times. (30 sc)

ROUND 25: Sc in each sc around. (30 sc)

ROUND 26: [Sc in each of next 3 sc, sc-dec] 6 times. (24 sc)

ROUNDS 27-30: Sc in each sc around. (24 sc) Fasten off.

Skirt - First Frill

ROUND 1: Holding the Body/Dress upside down, working in the unused front loops on Round 9, using Color C, **join with sc** (see Techniques) to any sc, [sc in next sc] around. DO NOT JOIN. (60 sc) Mark last stitch.

ROUND 2: [Hdc in next sc, 2 hdc in next sc] around. (90 hdc) Move marker each round.

ROUNDS 3-6: Hdc in each hdc around. (90 hdc)
At the end of Round 6, sc in next hdc, sl st in next hdc. Fasten off and weave in all ends.

Skirt - Second Frill

ROUNDS 1-2: Using Color B and Working in unused front loops on Round 11, repeat Rounds 1-2 of First Frill.

ROUNDS 3-5: Hdc in each hdc around. (90 hdc)
At the end of Round 5, sc in next hdc, sl st in next hdc. Fasten off and weave in all ends.

- Finish stuffing Body and Head.

- Using yarn needle and long tail from Head, sew Head to Body, matching stitches, and making sure neck is firmly stuffed to support the Head.

ARMS (Make 2)

ROUNDS 1-3: Using Color A, repeat Rounds 1-3 of Head.
At the end of Round 3, there are 18 sc.

ROUND 4: [Sc in each of next 8 sc, inc in next sc] twice. (20 sc)

ROUNDS 5-8: Sc in each sc around. (20 sc)

ROUND 9: [Sc in each of next 8 sc, sc-dec] twice. (18 sc)

- Start stuffing Arm, adding more as you go.

ROUNDS 10-26: Sc in each sc around. (18 sc) Fasten off.

SLEEVES (make 2)

ROUNDS 1-3: Using Color B and starting with a long tail on right side, repeat Rounds 1-3 of Head.
At the end of Round 3, there are 18 sc.

ROUNDS 4-10: Sc in each sc around. (18 sc)
At the end of Round 10, DO NOT FASTEN OFF.

- Stuff Sleeve firmly.

Joining Round: Holding the Sleeve towards you and working in both the Sleeve and the last Round of the Arm together, matching stitches, sc in each sc around, adding more stuffing if necessary. (18 sc) Fasten off and weave in all ends.

- Using starting tail of Sleeve and yarn needle, position Arms on either side of Neck and sew in position.

BALLET SHOES (Make 2)

ROUNDS 1-6: Using Color E, repeat Rounds 1-6 of Head. At the end of Round 6, there are 36 sc.

ROUNDS 7-11: Sc in each sc around. (36 sc)

ROUND 12: Sc in each of next 14 sc, [sc-dec] 4 times, sc in each of next 14 sc. (32 sc)

ROUND 13: Sc in each of next 10 sc, [sc in next sc, sc-dec] 4 times, sc in each of next 10 sc. (28 sc)

ROUND 14: Sc in each of next 10 sc, ch 8, skip next 8 sc, sc in each of next 10 sc. (20 sc & ch-8 lp) Fasten off and weave in all ends.

- Place the Shoes on the Feet.

Designer's Note: The fit might be a bit tight, but it is possible to get the Shoes on.

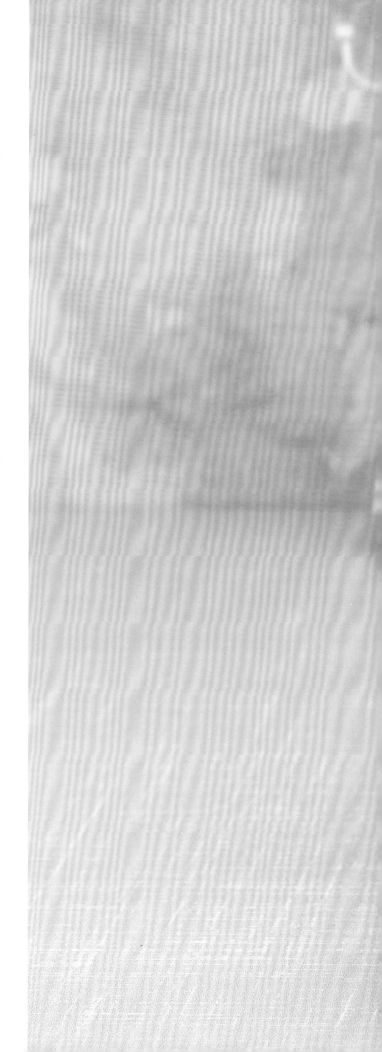

Spotty The Giraffe

By Tine Nielsen

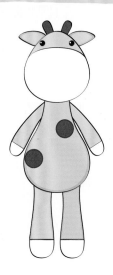

MATERIALS NEEDED

DMC Natura Just Cotton
Color A - Tournesol (N16)
Color B - Ivory (N02) for Hands, Feet and Face
Color C - Siena (N41) for Horns & Spots

Hook
Size C-2 (2.75 mm) or size suitable for yarn used.

Other
Polyester Fiberfill for stuffing
⅜" (10 mm) Safety Eyes - 2
Yarn Needle, sewing needle, scissors, stitch markers.

GIRAFFE

HEAD

ROUND 1: (Right Side) Using Color B, make a Magic Ring (see Techniques), 6 sc in ring. DO NOT JOIN. (6 sc) Mark last stitch.

ROUND 2: 2 sc in each sc around. (12 sc) Move marker each round.

ROUND 3: [Sc in next sc, **inc** (see Special Stitches) in next sc] around. (18 sc)

ROUND 4: [Sc in each of next 2 sc, inc in next sc] around. (24 sc)

ROUND 5: [Sc in each of next 3 sc, inc in next sc] around. (30 sc)

ROUND 6: [Sc in each of next 4 sc, inc in next sc] around. (36 sc)

ROUND 7: [Sc in each of next 5 sc, inc in next sc] around. (42 sc)

ROUND 8: [Sc in each of next 6 sc, inc in next sc] around. (48 sc)

ROUND 9: [Sc in each of next 7 sc, inc in next sc] around. (54 sc)

ROUND 10: [Sc in each of next 8 sc, inc in next sc] around. (60 sc)

ROUND 11: [Sc in each of next 9 sc, inc in next sc] around. (66 sc)

ROUNDS 12-21: Sc in each sc around. (66 sc)
At the end of Round 21, **change color** (see Techniques) to Color A in last st.

ROUND 22: Sc in each sc around. (66 sc)

ROUND 23: [Sc in each of next 9 sc, **sc-dec** (see Special Stitches)] around. (60 sc)

ROUNDS 24-25: Sc in each sc around. (60 sc)

ROUND 26: [Sc in each of next 8 sc, sc-dec] around. (54 sc)

ROUNDS 27-28: Sc in each sc around. (54 sc)

ROUND 29: [Sc in each of next 7 sc, sc-dec] around. (48 sc)

ROUNDS 30-31: Sc in each sc around. (48 sc)

ROUND 32: [Sc in each of next 6 sc, sc-dec] around. (42 sc)

ROUNDS 33-34: Sc in each sc around. (42 sc)

- Insert Safety Eyes between Rounds 27 & 28, with about 10 sts between them.

- Start stuffing the Head firmly, adding more as you go.

ROUND 35: [Sc in each of next 5 sc, sc-dec] around. (36 sc)

ROUND 36: Sc in each sc around. (36 sc)

ROUND 37: [Sc in each of next 4 sc, sc-dec] around. (30 sc)

ROUND 38: [Sc in each of next 3 sc, sc-dec] around. (24 sc)

ROUND 39: [Sc in each of next 2 sc, sc-dec] around. (18 sc)

ROUND 40: [Sc in next sc, sc-dec] around. (12 sc)

ROUND 41: [Sc-dec] around. (6 sc) Fasten off leaving long tail for sewing.

- Finish stuffing Head.

- Using yarn needle and long tail, **close the opening** (see Techniques).

EARS (Make 2)

ROUND 1: (Right Side) Using Color B, make a Magic Ring, 6 sc in ring. DO NOT JOIN. (6 sc) Mark last stitch.

ROUND 2: [Sc in next sc, inc in next sc] 3 times. (9 sc) Move marker each round.

ROUND 3: Sc in each sc around. (9 sc)

ROUND 4: [Sc in each of next 2 sc, inc in next sc] 3 times. (12 sc)

ROUNDS 5-6: Sc in each sc around. (12 sc)

ROUND 7: [Sc in next sc, inc in next sc] around. (18 sc)

ROUNDS 8-10: Sc in each sc around. (18 sc)

ROUND 11: [Sc in next sc, sc-dec] around. (12 sc) Fasten off leaving long tail for sewing.

- Do not stuff the Ears.

- Position the Ears between Rounds 33 & 35 of either side of Head and using long tail and yarn needle, sew in place.

HORNS (Make 2)

ROUND 1: (Right Side) Using Color C, make a Magic Ring, 8 sc in ring. DO NOT JOIN. (8 sc) Mark last stitch.

ROUNDS 2-5: Sc in each sc around. (8 sc) Move marker each round.

At the end of Round 5, fasten off leaving long tail for sewing.

- Stuff the Horns.

- Position the Horns on the Head between the Ears and using long tail and yarn needle, sew in place.

BODY

ROUNDS 1-11: Using Color A, repeat Rounds 1-11 of Head. At the end of Round 11, there are 66 sc.

ROUNDS 12-24: Sc in each sc around. (66 sc)

ROUND 25: [Sc in each of next 9 sc, sc-dec] around. (60 sc)

ROUND 26: Sc in each sc around. (60 sc)

ROUND 27: [Sc in each of next 8 sc, sc-dec] around. (54 sc)

ROUND 28: Sc in each sc around. (54 sc)

ROUND 29: [Sc in each of next 7 sc, sc-dec] around. (48 sc)

ROUNDS 30-31: Sc in each sc around. (48 sc)

ROUND 32: [Sc in each of next 6 sc, sc-dec] around. (42 sc)

ROUNDS 33-34: Sc in each sc around. (42 sc)

- Start stuffing the Body firmly, adding more as you go.

ROUND 35: [Sc in each of next 5 sc, sc-dec] around. (36 sc)

ROUNDS 36-37: Sc in each sc around. (36 sc)

ROUND 38: [Sc in each of next 4 sc, sc-dec] around. (30 sc)

ROUNDS 39-45: Sc in each sc around. (30 sc)

ROUND 46: Sc in each of next 7 sc, hdc in each of next 16 sc, sc in each of next 7 sc. (30 sts) Fasten off leaving long tail for sewing.

- Finish stuffing Body.

- Position Head on Body (with the hdc-sts of last round of Body at the back of the neck).

- Using yarn needle and long tail, sew Body to Head, stuffing the Neck firmly.

ARMS (Make 2)

ROUNDS 1-2: Using Color B, repeat Rounds 1-2 of Head. At the end of Round 2, there are 12 sc.

ROUND 3: [Sc in each of next 2 sc, inc in next sc] around. (16 sc)

ROUNDS 4-5: Sc in each sc around. (16 sc) At the end of Round 5, change color to Color A in last st.

ROUNDS 6-10: With Color A, sc in each sc around. (16 sc)

ROUND 11: [Sc in each of next 6 sc, sc-dec] twice. (14 sc)

- Start stuffing the Arms, adding more as you go.

ROUNDS 12-23: Sc in each sc around. (14 sc)

At the end of Round 23, fasten off leaving long tail for sewing.

- Finish stuffing the bottom of the Arms, but do not stuff the top.

- Flatten the last round and position the Arms on either side of the Body at about Round 40.

- Using long tail and yarn needle, sew Arms in place.

LEGS (Make 2)

ROUNDS 1-5: Using Color B, repeat Rounds 1-5 of Head. At the end of Round 5, there are 30 sc.

ROUNDS 6-9: Sc in each sc around. (30 sc) At the end of Round 9, change color to Color A in last st.

ROUNDS 10-11: With Color A, sc in each sc around. (30 sc)

ROUND 12: [Sc in each of next 13 sc, sc-dec] twice. (28 sc)

ROUNDS 13-15: Sc in each sc around. (28 sc)

- Start stuffing the Legs, adding more as you go.

ROUND 16: [Sc in each of next 12 sc, sc-dec] twice. (26 sc)

ROUNDS 17-19: Sc in each sc around. (26 sc)

ROUND 20: [Sc in each of next 11 sc, sc-dec] twice. (24 sc)

ROUNDS 21-23: Sc in each sc around. (24 sc)

ROUND 24: [Sc in each of next 10 sc, sc-dec] twice. (22 sc)

ROUNDS 25-27: Sc in each sc around. (22 sc)

ROUND 28: [Sc in each of next 9 sc, sc-dec] twice. (20 sc)

ROUNDS 29-31: Sc in each sc around. (20 sc)

ROUND 32: [Sc in each of next 8 sc, sc-dec] twice. (18 sc) Fasten off leaving long tail for sewing.

- Finish stuffing the bottom of the Legs, but do not stuff the top.

- Flatten the last round and position the Legs on the bottom of the Body, so that the Giraffe can sit.

- Using long tail and yarn needle, sew Legs in place.

SPOTS

Small Spots (make 3)

ROUNDS 1-2: Using Color C, repeat Rounds 1-2 of Head. At the end of Round 2, there are 12 sc. Fasten off using **Invisible Join** (see Techniques), leaving long tail for sewing.

Large Spots (make 3)

ROUNDS 1-3: Using Color C, repeat Rounds 1-3 of Head. At the end of Round 3, there are 18 sc. Fasten off using Invisible Join, leaving long tail for sewing.

- Position the Spots randomly on the Body and using long tail and yarn needle, sew in place.

Designer's Note: If you like, you can crochet more Spots to sew on the Giraffe.

Sleepy Hippo

By Soledad Iglesias

FINISHED SIZE
About 11¾" (24 cm) long.

MATERIALS NEEDED

DMC Natura Just Cotton
Color A - Sable (N03) for Head & Body
Color B - Lobelia (N82) - for Nostrils, Dress Stripes & Ruffles
Color C - Ibiza (N01) - for Dress Stripes
Color D - Crimson (N61) - for Dress Stripes

Hook
Size B-1 (2.25 mm) or size suitable for yarn used.

Other
Polyester Fiberfill for stuffing
Black Embroidery Floss - for Eyes
Cosmetic Blusher (optional) - for Cheeks
Yarn Needle, sewing needle, scissors, stitch markers.

Gauge
36 sc & 36 sc rows = 4" (10 cm) square

HIPPO

HEAD

ROUND 1: (Right Side) Using Color A, ch 9, 2 sc in 2nd ch from hook, sc in each of next 6 ch, 3 sc in last ch, working in unused lps on other side of starting ch, sc in each of next 6 ch, sc in last ch (same ch as first 2-sc). DO NOT JOIN. (18 sc) Mark last stitch.

ROUND 2: Inc3 (see Special Stitches) in next sc, **inc** (see Special Stitches) in next sc, sc in each of next 6 sc, inc in next sc, inc3 in next sc, inc in next sc, sc in each of next 6 sc, inc in next sc. (26 sc) Move marker each round.

ROUND 3: [Inc in next sc, sc in next sc] twice, sc in each of next 7 sc, [inc in next sc, sc in next sc] 3 times, sc in each of next 7 sc, inc in next sc, sc in next sc. (32 sc)

ROUND 4: Sc in each of next 2 sc, [inc in next sc] twice, sc in each of next 2 sc, inc in next sc, sc in each of next 8 sc, inc in next sc, sc in each of next 2 sc, [inc in next sc] twice, sc in each of next 2 sc, inc in next sc, sc in each of next 8 sc, inc in next sc. (40 sc)

ROUND 5: Inc in next sc, sc in each of next 2 sc, inc in next sc, sc in each of next 3 sc, inc in next sc, sc in each of next 8 sc, inc in next sc, sc in each of next 3 sc, inc in next sc, sc in each of next 2 sc, inc in next sc, sc in each of next 3 sc, inc in next sc, sc in each of next 8 sc, inc in next sc, sc in each of next 3 sc. (48 sc)

ROUND 6: [Inc in next sc, sc in each of next 4 sc] twice, inc in next sc, sc in each of next 8 sc, [inc in next sc, sc in each of next 4 sc] 3 times, inc in next sc, sc in each of next 8 sc, inc in next sc, sc in each of next 4 sc. (56 sc)

ROUND 7: [Inc in next sc, sc in each of next 4 sc] 3 times, inc in next sc, sc in each of next 10 sc, [inc in next sc, sc in each of next 4 sc] 3 times, inc in next sc, sc in each of next 14 sc. (64 sc)

ROUNDS 8-9: Sc in each sc around. (64 sc)

ROUND 10: [Inc in next sc, sc in each of next 5 sc] 3 times, inc in next sc, sc in each of next 12 sc, [inc in next sc, sc in each of next 5 sc] 3 times, inc in next sc, sc in each of next 14 sc. (72 sc)

ROUND 11: Sc in each sc around. (72 sc)

ROUND 12: [Inc in next sc, sc in each of next 5 sc] 3 times, inc in next sc, sc in each of next 16 sc, [inc in next sc, sc in each of next 5 sc] 3 times, inc in next sc, sc in each of next 18 sc. (80 sc)

ROUND 13: Sc in each sc around. (80 sc)

ROUND 14: Sc in each of next 3 sc, [inc in next sc, sc in each of next 5 sc] 3 times, inc in next sc, sc in each of next 20 sc, [inc in next sc, sc in each of next 5 sc] 3 times, inc in next sc, sc in each of next 19 sc. (88 sc)

ROUND 15: Sc in each sc around. (88 sc)

ROUND 16: [Sc in each of next 10 sc, inc in next sc] 8 times. (96 sc)

ROUNDS 17-18: Sc in each sc around. (96 sc)

ROUND 19: [Sc in each of next 10 sc, **sc-dec** (see Special Stitches)] 8 times. (88 sc)

ROUND 20: Sc in each sc around. (88 sc)

ROUND 21: [Sc in each of next 9 sc, sc-dec] 8 times. (80 sc)

ROUND 22: Sc in each sc around. (80 sc)

ROUND 23: [Sc in each of next 8 sc, sc-dec] 8 times. (72 sc)

ROUND 24: Sc in each sc around. (72 sc)

ROUND 25: [Sc in each of next 7 sc, sc-dec] 8 times. (64 sc)

ROUNDS 26-27: Sc in each sc around. (64 sc)

ROUND 28: [Sc in each of next 6 sc, sc-dec] 8 times. (56 sc)

ROUND 29: [Sc in each of next 5 sc, sc-dec] 8 times. (48 sc)

ROUNDS 30-39: Sc in each sc around. (48 sc)

- Start stuffing Head firmly, adding more as you go.

ROUND 40: [Sc in each of next 4 sc, sc-dec] 8 times. (40 sc)

ROUND 41: [Sc in each of next 3 sc, sc-dec] 8 times. (32 sc)

ROUND 42: [Sc in each of next 2 sc, sc-dec] 8 times. (24 sc)

ROUND 43: [Sc in next sc, sc-dec] 8 times. (16 sc)

ROUND 44: [Sc-dec] 8 times. (8 sc) Fasten off leaving long tail for sewing.

- Finish stuffing Head.

- Using long tail and yarn needle, **close the opening** (see Techniques).

- Using floss, embroider the Eyes using small **Back Stitches** (see Embroidery Stitches) between Rounds 21 & 22, with 9 stitches between them.

NOSTRILS (Make 2)

ROUND 1: (Right Side) Using Color B, make a **Magic Ring** (see Techniques), 6 sc in ring; join with sl st to first sc. (6 sc) Fasten off with **invisible join** (see Techniques) leaving long tail for sewing.

- Using long tails and yarn needle, sew the Nostrils between Rounds 15 & 17 (beneath each Eye) with 14 stitches between them.

EARS (Make 2)

ROUND 1: (Right Side) Using Color A, make a Magic Ring, 6 sc in ring. DO NOT JOIN. (6 sc) Mark last stitch.

ROUND 2: 2 sc in each sc around. (12 sc) Move marker each round.

ROUND 3: [Sc in next sc, inc in next sc] around. (18 sc) Place another marker in the 3rd last sc of Round.

ROW 4: [Sc in each of next 2 sc, inc in next sc] 3 times. (12 sc) Fold the Ear in half, aligning the marked sc (3rd last st) with the next sc, working through both thicknesses, sc in each of next 3 sc. Fasten off leaving long tail for sewing.

- Using long tail and yarn needle, sew the Ears on either side of the Head at Round 38.

- Apply blusher to the cheeks.

BODY

ROUND 1: (Right Side) Using Color A, make a Magic Ring, 8 sc in ring. DO NOT JOIN. (8 sc) Mark last stitch.

ROUND 2: 2 sc in each sc around. (16 sc) Move marker each round.

ROUND 3: [Sc in next sc, inc in next sc] around. (24 sc)

ROUND 4: [Sc in each of next 2 sc, inc in next sc] around. (32 sc)

ROUND 5: [Sc in each of next 3 sc, inc in next sc] around. (40 sc)

ROUND 6: [Sc in each of next 4 sc, inc in next sc] around. (48 sc)

ROUND 7: [Sc in each of next 5 sc, inc in next sc] around. (56 sc)

ROUND 8: [Sc in each of next 6 sc, inc in next sc] around. (64 sc)

ROUND 9: [Sc in each of next 7 sc, inc in next sc] around. (72 sc)

ROUND 10: [Sc in each of next 8 sc, inc in next sc] around. (80 sc)

ROUND 11: [Sc in each of next 9 sc, inc in next sc] around. (88 sc)

ROUND 12: [Sc in each of next 10 sc, inc in next sc] around. (96 sc)

ROUNDS 13-26: Sc in each sc around. (96 sc)

At the end of Round 26, **change color** (see Techniques) to Color B.

ROUND 27: With Color B, working in **back loops** only (see Techniques), sc in each sc around, changing to Color C in last st. (96 sc)

Continue working in both loops of stitches.

ROUND 28: With Color C, sc in each sc around, changing to Color D in last st. (96 sc)

ROUND 29: With Color D, sc in each sc around, changing to Color C in last st. (96 sc)

ROUND 30: With Color C, sc in each sc around, changing to Color B in last st. (96 sc)

ROUND 31: With Color B, sc in each sc around, changing to Color C in last st. (96 sc)

ROUNDS 32-35: Repeat rounds 28-31 once more. (96 sc)

ROUND 36: With Color C, sc in each sc around, changing to Color D in last st. (96 sc)

ROUND 37: With Color D, [sc in each of next 4 sc, sc-dec] 8 times, sc in each of next 48 sc, changing to Color C in last st. (88 sc)

ROUND 38: With Color C, [sc in each of next 3 sc, sc-dec] 8 times, sc in each of next 48 sc, changing to Color B in last st. (80 sc)

ROUND 39: With Color B, [sc in each of next 2 sc, sc-dec] 8 times, sc in each of next 48 sc, changing to Color C in last st. (72 sc)

ROUNDS 40-42: Repeat rounds 28-30 once. (72 sc)

- Start stuffing the Body, adding more as you go.

ROUND 43: With Color B, [sc in each of next 7 sc, sc-dec] around, changing to Color C in last st. (64 sc)

ROUND 44: With Color C, sc in each sc around, changing to Color D in last st. (64 sc)

ROUND 45: With Color D, [sc in each of next 6 sc, sc-dec] around, changing to Color C in last st. (56 sc)

ROUND 46: With Color C, sc in each sc around, changing to Color B in last st. (56 sc)

ROUND 47: With Color B, [sc in each of next 5 sc, sc-dec] around, changing to Color A in last st. (48 sc)

ROUND 48: With Color A, sc in each sc around. (48 sc) Fasten off leaving long tail for sewing.

Body Ruffle

ROUND 1: Holding the Body upside down, working in unused front loops on Round 26, using Color B, **join with sc** (see Techniques) to any st, sc in same st, [2 sc in next st] around; join with sl st to first sc. (192 sc)

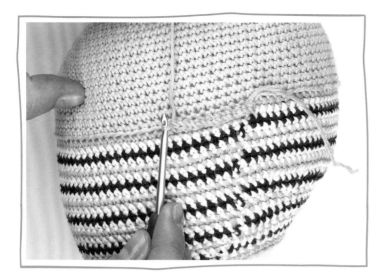

ROUND 2: Ch 1, sc in each sc around; join with sl st to first sc. (192 sc) Fasten off and weave in all ends.

- Finish stuffing the Body.
- With the flat part of the Body to the front, position Body between Round 13 & 26 of Head.
- Using long tail and yarn needle, sew in place.

ARMS (Make 2)

ROUND 1: (Right Side) Using Color A, make a Magic Ring, 6 sc in ring. DO NOT JOIN. (6 sc) Mark last stitch.

ROUND 2: 2 sc in each sc around. (12 sc) Move marker each round.

ROUND 3: [Sc in next sc, inc in next sc] around. (18 sc)

ROUND 4: [Sc in each of next 2 sc, inc in next sc] around. (24 sc)

ROUND 5: [Sc in each of next 3 sc, inc in next sc] around. (30 sc)

ROUND 6: [Sc in each of next 4 sc, inc in next sc] around. (36 sc)

ROUND 7: Working in **back loops** only, sc in each sc around. (36 sc)

ROUNDS 8-11: Working in both loops, sc in each sc around. (36 sc)

ROUND 12: [Sc-dec] twice, sc in each of next 12 sc, [inc in next sc] 4 times, sc in each of next 12 sc, [sc-dec] twice. (36 sc)

ROUNDS 13-16: Sc in each sc around. (36 sc)

ROUND 17: Repeat Round 12. (36 sc)

ROUNDS 18-22: Sc in each sc around. (36 sc)

ROUND 23: [Sc in each of next 4 sc, sc-dec] around. (30 sc)

ROUNDS 24-29: Sc in each sc around. (30 sc)

At the end of Round 29, change color to Color B.

ROUND 30: With Color B, working in **back loops** only, sc in each sc around, changing to Color C in last st. (30 sc)

Continue working in both loops of stitches.

ROUND 31: With Color C, sc in each sc around, changing to Color D in last st. (30 sc)

ROUND 32: With Color D, sc in each sc around, changing to Color C in last st. (30 sc)

- Start stuffing the Arms firmly.

Work continues in Rows.

For Right Arm Only:

ROW 33: With Color C, (do not turn- right side facing), sc in each of next 16 sc, changing to Color B in last st. (16 sc) Leave remaining sts unworked.

For Left Arm Only:

ROW 33: With Color C, turn (wrong side facing), sc in each of next 16 sc, changing to Color B in last st. (16 sc) Leave remaining sts unworked.

For Both Arms:

ROW 34: With Color B, turn, skip first sc, sc in each of next 14 sc, changing to Color C in last st. (14 sc) Leave remaining sc unworked.

ROW 35: With Color C, turn, skip first sc, sc in each of next 12 sc, changing to Color D in last st. (12 sc) Leave remaining sc unworked.

ROW 36: With Color D, skip first sc, sc in each of next 10 sc, changing to Color C in last st. (10 sc) Leave remaining sc unworked.

ROW 37: With Color C, turn, skip first sc, sc in each of next 8 sc, changing to Color B in last st. (8 sc) Leave remaining sc unworked.

ROW 38: With Color B, turn, skip first sc, sc in each of next 6 sc, changing to Color C in last st. (6 sc) Leave remaining sc unworked.

ROW 39: With Color C, skip first sc, sc in each of next 4 sc, changing to Color D in last st. (4 sc) Leave remaining sc unworked.

ROW 40: With Color D, turn, skip the first sc, sc in each of next 2 sc, changing to Color C in last st. (2 sc) Leave remaining sc unworked.

ROUND 41: With Color C, turn, skip the first sc, sc in next sc, working in skipped sts, sc in each of next 8 sc, working in unworked stitches on Round 32, sc in each of next 14 sc, working in skipped sts, sc in each of next 8 sc; join with sl st to first sc. (30 sc) Fasten off leaving long tail for sewing.

Arm Ruffle

ROUND 1: Holding the Arm upside down, working in unused front loops on Round 29, using Color B, join with sc to any st, sc in same st, [2 sc in next st] around; join with sl st to first sc. (60 sc)

ROUND 2: Ch 1, sc in each sc around; join with sl st to first sc. (60 sc) Fasten off and weave in all ends.

Repeat for other Arm.
- Using photo as guide, position the Arms between

Rounds 37 & 47 of Body.

- Using long tail and yarn needle, sew Arms in place, stuffing as you go.

LEGS (Make 2)

ROUND 1: (Right Side) Using Color A, ch 7, 2 sc in 2ⁿᵈ ch from hook, sc in each of next 4 ch, 3 sc in last ch, working in unused lps on other side of starting ch, sc in each of next 4 ch, sc in last ch (same ch as first 2-sc); join with sl st to first sc. (14 sc)

ROUND 2: Ch 1, inc in first sc, sc in each of next 5 sc, [inc in next sc] 3 times, sc in each of next 4 sc, inc3 in next sc; join with sl st to first sc. (20 sc)

ROUND 3: Ch 1, sc in first sc, sc in each of next 6 sc, [inc in next sc] 5 times, sc in each of next 7 sc, inc3 in next sc; join with sl st to first sc. (27 sc)

ROUND 4: Ch 1, sc in first sc, sc in each of next 9 sc, [inc in next sc] 4 times, sc in each of next 11 sc, inc in next sc, sc in last sc; join with sl st to first sc. (32 sc)

ROUND 5: Ch 1, sc in first sc, sc in each of next 8 sc, [inc in next sc] twice, sc in each of next 6 sc, [inc in next sc] twice, sc in each of next 10 sc, [inc in next sc] twice, sc in last sc; join with sl st to first sc. (38 sc)

ROUND 6: Ch 1, sc in first sc, sc in each of next 9 sc, *inc in next sc, sc in next sc, inc in next sc*, sc in each of next 6 sc; rep from * to * once, sc in each of next 12 sc, [inc in next sc] twice, sc in each of last 2 sc; join with sl st to first sc. (44 sc)

ROUND 7: Ch 1, sc in first sc, sc in each of next 11 sc, inc in next sc, sc in each of next 10 sc, inc in next sc, sc in each of next 15 sc, [inc in next sc] twice, sc in each of last 3 sc; join with sl st to first sc. (48 sc)

ROUND 8: Ch 1, sc in first sc, sc in each of next 13 sc, *inc in next sc, sc in each of next 2 sc, inc in next sc*, sc in each of next 6 sc; rep from * to * once, sc in each of next 17 sc, [inc in next sc] twice, sc in last sc; join with sl st to first sc. (54 sc)

ROUND 9: Ch 1, sc in first sc, sc in each of next 14 sc, *inc in next sc, sc in each of next 2 sc, inc in next sc*, sc in each of next 7 sc; rep from * to * once, sc in each of next 19 sc, [inc in next sc, sc in next sc] twice, sc in last sc; join with sl st to first sc. (60 sc) Mark last stitch worked.

Work continues in spiral.

ROUND 10: Ch 1, sc in each sc around. (60 sc) DO NOT JOIN. Move marker each round.

ROUNDS 11-14: Sc in each sc around. (60 sc)

ROUND 15: Sc in each of next 16 sc, [sc-dec] 5 times, sc in each of next 2 sc, [sc-dec] 5 times, sc in each of next 12 sc, sc-dec, sc in each of next 6 sc, sc-dec. (48 sc)

ROUND 16: [Sc in each of next 6 sc, sc-dec] around. (42 sc)

ROUND 17: [Sc in each of next 5 sc, sc-dec] around. (36 sc)

ROUNDS 18-19: Sc in each sc around. (36 sc)

- Start stuffing Leg, adding more as you go.

ROUND 20: [Sc in each of next 5 sc, inc in next sc] around. (42 sc)

ROUND 21: [Sc in each of next 6 sc, inc in next sc] around. (48 sc)

ROUNDS 22-24: Sc in each sc around. (48 sc)

At the end of Round 24, work continues in Rows.

ROW 25: (Do not turn.) Sc in each of next 46 sc. (46 sc) Leave remaining sts unworked.

ROWS 26-37: Turn, skip first sc, sc in each sc across to 2ⁿᵈ last sc. Leave remaining sc unworked.

At the end of Row 37, there are 20 sc.

ROUND 38: Turn, sc in first sc, sc in each of next 19 sc, working in skipped sts, sc in each of next 13 sc, working in unworked stitches on Round 23, sc in each of next 2 sc, working in skipped sts, sc in each of next 13 sc; join with sl st to first sc. (48 sc) Fasten off leaving long tail for sewing.

- Position the Legs at base of Body.

- Using long tail and yarn needle, sew Legs in place, stuffing as you go.

TAIL

ROUND 1: (Right Side) Starting with 8" (20 cm) long tail for sewing, using Color A, ch 12, taking care not to twist chain, sl st in first ch to form ring; 12 sc in ring; DO NOT JOIN. (12 sc) Mark last stitch.

ROUNDS 2-3: Sc in each sc around. (12 sc) Move marker each round.

ROUND 4: [Sc in next sc, sc-dec] around. (8 sc)

ROUNDS 5-7: Sc in each sc around. (8 sc)

ROUND 8: [Sc-dec] around. (4 sc)

ROUNDS 9-10: Sc in each sc around. (4 sc)

At the end of Round 10, fasten off leaving long tail.

- Using yarn needle and long tail, **close the opening** (see Techniques).

- Position the Tail between the Legs at about Round 11 of Body. Using yarn needle and starting tail, sew Tail in place.

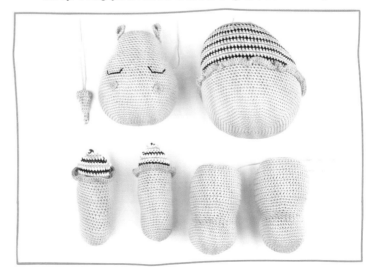

Shellie The Tortoise

By Soledad Iglesias

FINISHED SIZE
Large Tortoise - about 13½"(34 cm) tall.
Small Tortoise - about 10" (25,5 cm) tall.

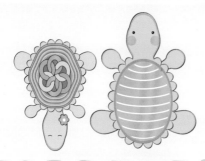

MATERIALS NEEDED

For Large Tortoise

DMC Natura Medium Just Cotton
Color A - Lime Green (#198) for Head and Limbs
Color B - Rust Orange (#109)
Color C - Khaki (#89)
Color D - White (#01) - for Belly Stripes

For Small Tortoise

DMC Natura Just Cotton Yummy
Color A - Visir (N96) for Head and Limbs
Color B - Rose de Meaux (N94)

DMC Natura Just Cotton
Color C - Chartreuse (N48)
Color D - Ivory (N02) - for Belly Stripes and Small Flower

Hook
For Larger Tortoise - Size G-6 (4.00 mm) or size suitable for yarn used.
For Smaller Tortoise - Size D-3 (3.25 mm) or size suitable for yarn used.

Other
Polyester Fiberfill for stuffing
Safety Eyes ¼" (6 mm) - 2 (sitting version)
Black Embroidery Floss - for Eyes (sleeping version)
Cosmetic Blusher (optional) - for cheeks
Yarn Needle, sewing needle, scissors, stitch markers.

Gauge (using larger hook)
20 sc & 20 sc rows = 4" (10 cm) square

Designer's Note
The same pattern is used for both the
Large and Small Tortoise.

TORTOISE

ADDITIONAL STITCHES USED IN PATTERN

Surface Stitches: With right side facing, make a slip knot; insert hook at beginning of Row into Belly cavity, place slip knot on hook and bring loop to front of work, keeping yarn at back, *insert hook in next stitch (into cavity), pull up yarn through fabric and through loop on hook (slip stitch); rep from * across row.

Popcorn (pop): Work 3 double crochets in the same stitch specified, remove hook from loop, insert hook from front to back through the top of first dc made, place loop back on hook and pull dropped loop through stitch.

OUTER SHELL (Interlocking Rings)

Color A – First and Fourth Ring
Color B – Second and Fifth Ring
Color C – Third and Sixth Ring

First Ring: (Right Side) Using Color A, ch 13; taking care not to twist chain, join with sl st to first ch to form ring; ch 3 (counts as first dc, now and throughout), 29 dc in ring; join with sl st to first dc (3rd ch of beg ch-3) and cut yarn or fasten off with **invisible join** (see Techniques). (30 dc)

Second to Fifth Ring: (Right Side) Using next Color, ch 13; with right side of previous Ring facing, insert current chain through center of previous Ring, taking care not to twist chain, join with sl st to first ch to form ring; ch 3 (counts as first dc, now and throughout), 29 dc in ring; join with sl st to first dc (3rd ch of beg ch-3) and cut yarn or fasten off with invisible join.. (30 dc)

Sixth Ring: (Right Side) Using Color C, ch 13; with right side of previous Ring facing, insert current chain through center of previous Ring and through center of First Ring, taking care not to twist chain, join with sl st to first ch to form ring; ch 3 (counts as first dc, now and throughout), 29 dc in ring; join with sl st to first dc (3rd ch of beg ch-3) and cut yarn or fasten off with invisible join.. (30 dc)

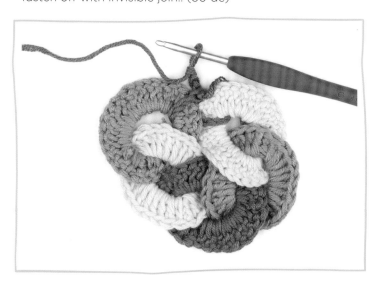

TOP OF SHELL

ROUND 1: (Right Side) Using Color C, make a **Magic Ring** (see Techniques), 6 sc in ring. DO NOT JOIN. (6 sc) Mark last stitch.

ROUND 2: 2 sc in each sc around. (12 sc) Move marker each round.

ROUND 3: [Sc in next sc, **inc** (see Special Stitches) in next sc] around. (18 sc)

ROUND 4: [Sc in each of next 2 sc, inc in next sc] around. (24 sc)

ROUND 5: [Sc in each of next 3 sc, inc in next sc] around. (30 sc)

ROUND 6: [Sc in each of next 4 sc, inc in next sc] around. (36 sc)

ROUND 7: [Sc in each of next 5 sc, inc in next sc] around. (42 sc)

ROUND 8: [Sc in each of next 6 sc, inc in next sc] around. (48 sc)

ROUND 9: [Sc in each of next 7 sc, inc in next sc] around. (54 sc)

ROUND 10: Holding the finished Outer Shell in front (right side facing you), working through both thicknesses, aligning dc-sts on edge of Outer Shell with sc sts behind, working in each Ring, [sc in each of next 9 dc] in each Ring around, **changing color** (see Techniques) to Color B in last st; with Color B, join with sl st to first sc. (54 sc) Do not cut Color C.

ROUND 11: With Color B, ch 1, sc in same st as joining, sc in each of next 7 sc, inc in next sc, [sc in each of next 8 sc, inc in next sc] around, change to Color A; with Color A, join with sl st to first sc. (60 sc) Do not cut Color B.

ROUND 12: Ch 1, sc in same st as joining, sc in each of next 8 sc, inc in next sc, [sc in each of next 9 sc, inc in next sc] around, change to Color C; with Color C, join with sl st to first sc. (66 sc) Do not cut Color A.

ROUND 13: Ch 1, sc in same st as joining, sc in each of next 9 sc, inc in next sc, [sc in each of next 10 sc, inc in next sc] around, change to Color B; with Color B, join with sl st to first sc. (72 sc) Do not cut Color C.

ROUND 14: Ch 1, sc in same st as joining, sc in each of next 10 sc, inc in next sc, [sc in each of next 11 sc, inc in next sc] around, change to Color A; with Color A, join with sl st to first sc. (78 sc) Do not cut Color B.

ROUND 15: Ch 1, sc in same st as joining, sc in each of next 11 sc, inc in next sc, [sc in each of next 12 sc, inc in next sc] around, change to Color C; with Color C, join with sl st to first sc. (84 sc) Do not cut Color A.

ROUND 16: Ch 1, sc in same st as joining, sc in each of next 12 sc, inc in next sc, [sc in each of next 13 sc, inc in next sc] around, change to Color B; with Color B, join with sl st to first sc. (90 sc) Do not cut Color C.

ROUND 17: Ch 1, sc in same st as joining, sc in each of next 13 sc, inc in next sc, [sc in each of next 14 sc, inc in next sc] around, change to Color A; with Color A, join with sl st to first sc. (96 sc) Do not cut Color B.

ROUND 18: Ch 1, sc in same st as joining, sc in each of next 14 sc, inc in next sc, [sc in each of next 15 sc, inc in next sc] around, change to Color C; with Color C, join with sl st to first sc. (102 sc) Do not cut Color A.

ROUND 19: Ch 1, sc in same st as joining, sc in each of next 15 sc, inc in next sc, [sc in each of next 16 sc, inc in next sc] around, change to Color B; with Color B, join with sl st to first sc. (108 sc) Cut Color C and weave in ends.

ROUND 20: Ch 1, sc in same st as joining, sc in each of next 16 sc, inc in next sc, [sc in each of next 17 sc, inc in next sc] around, change to Color A; with Color A, join with sl st to first sc. (114 sc) Cut Color B and weave in ends.

ROUND 21: Ch 1, sc in same st as joining, sc in each of next 17 sc, inc in next sc, [sc in each of next 18 sc, inc in next sc] around; join with sl st to first sc. (120 sc)

ROUND 22 (Edging): Ch 1, working in **front loops only** (see Techniques) for the whole round, sc in same st as joining, [skip next 2 sc, 9 tr in next sc, skip next 2 sc, sc in next sc] around, omitting last sc on final repeat; join with sl st to first sc. (20 sc & 20 shells) Fasten off and weave in all ends.

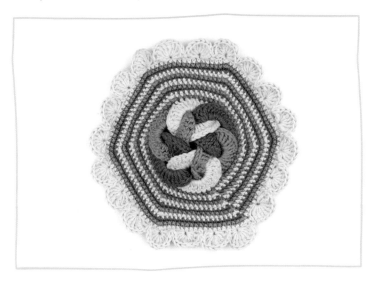

SHELL BELLY

ROW 1: (Right Side) With wrong side of Top of Shell facing, working in the unused back loops of Round 21, using Color B, **join with sc** (see Techniques) to any sc, working in back loops only, sc in each of next 21 sc. (22 sc) Leave remaining sts unworked.

ROW 2: Turn, skip the first sc, working in back loops only, sc in each of next 21 sc, working in Round 21, sc in each of next 2 sc. (23 sc)

ROWS 3-12: Turn, skip the first sc, working in back loops only, [sc in next sc] across, working in Round 21, sc in each of next 2 sc. At the end of Row 12, there are 33 sc.

ROWS 13-32: Turn, skip first 2 sc, working in back loops only, sc in each of next 31 sc, working in Round 21, sc in each of next 2 sc. (33 sc)

ROW 33: Turn, skip first 2 sc, working in back loops only, sc in each of next 29 sc, skip next sc, sc in last sc, working in Round 21, sc in each of next 2 sc. (32 sc)

ROWS 34-39: Turn, skip first 2 sc, working in back loops only, [sc in next sc] across to second last sc, skip next sc, sc in last sc, working in Round 21, sc in each of next 2 sc.

At the end of Row 39, there are 26 sc. (22 unused loops remaining on Round 21.) Fasten off Color B and weave in all ends.

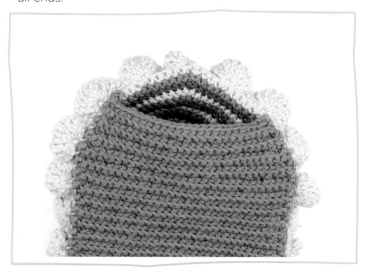

NECK & HEAD

ROUND 1: (Right Side) With right side of Belly facing, working in Row 39, using Color A, join with sc to back loop of first sc, working in **back loops** only (see Techniques), sc in each of next 25 sc, working in unused loops of Round 21, sc in each of next 22 sc. DO NOT JOIN. (48 sc) Remove hook and place stitch marker in loop.

Belly Stripes

First Stripe: With right side of Belly facing, working in unused front loops of Row 39, join Color D with sl st to front loop of first sc, sl st in each of next 25 sc. Fasten off Color D.

Remaining Stripes: Using Color D, work rows of **Surface Stitches** (see Additional Stitches) across Belly, every four rows.

NECK & HEAD (continued)

- After working the Belly Stripes, stuff the Belly firmly.

- Remove stitch marker from loop and mark last stitch made on Round 1. Work continues in a spiral.

ROUND 2: [Sc in each of next 6 sc, **sc-dec** (see Techniques)] around. (42 sc) Move marker each round.

ROUND 3: [Sc in each of next 5 sc, sc-dec] around. (36 sc)

ROUND 4: [Sc in each of next 4 sc, sc-dec] around. (30 sc)

ROUND 5: [Sc in each of next 3 sc, sc-dec] around. (24 sc)

ROUNDS 6-7: Sc in each sc around. (24 sc)

ROUND 8: [Sc in each of next 3 sc, inc in next sc] around. (30 sc)

ROUND 9: [Sc in each of next 4 sc, inc in next sc] around. (36 sc)

ROUND 10: [Sc in each of next 5 sc, inc in next sc] around. (42 sc)

ROUND 11: [Sc in each of next 6 sc, inc in next sc] around. (48 sc)

ROUNDS 12-20: Sc in each sc around. (48 sc)

ROUND 21: [Sc in each of next 6 sc, sc-dec] around. (42 sc)

ROUND 22: [Sc in each of next 5 sc, sc-dec] around. (36 sc)

For the sitting version of the Tortoise:
- Insert Safety Eyes between Rounds 20 & 21, with about 12 stitches between them.

For both versions:
- Start stuffing Neck and Head firmly, adding more as you go.

ROUNDS 23-27: Sc in each sc around. (36 sc)

ROUND 28: [Sc in each of next 4 sc, sc-dec] around. (30 sc)

ROUND 29: [Sc in each of next 3 sc, sc-dec] around. (24 sc)

ROUND 30: [Sc in each of next 2 sc, sc-dec] around. (18 sc)

ROUND 31: [Sc in next sc, sc-dec] around. (12 sc)

ROUND 32: [Sc-dec] around. (6 sc) Fasten off leaving long tail for sewing.

- Using yarn needle and long tail, **close the opening** (see Techniques).

For the sleeping version of the Tortoise:
- Using floss, embroider the Eyes using small **Bullion Stitches** (see Embroidery Stitches).

- Apply blusher to the cheeks.

SMALL FLOWER

ROUND 1: (Right Side) Using Color D, make a Magic Ring, 6 sc in ring, changing to color B in last st. DO NOT JOIN. (6 sc) Mark last stitch.

ROUND 2: With Color B, [ch 3, **pop** (see Additional Stitches) in same sc, ch 3, sl st in next sc] around. Fasten off leaving long tail for sewing.

- Position Flower on Head and using long tail and yarn needle, sew in place.

ARMS (Make 2)

ROUND 1: (Right Side) Using Color A, make a Magic Ring, 6 sc in ring. DO NOT JOIN. (6 sc) Mark last stitch.

ROUND 2: 2 sc in each sc around. (12 sc) Move marker each round.

ROUND 3: [Sc in each of next 3 sc, **inc3** (see Special Stitches) in next sc] 3 times. (18 sc)

ROUNDS 4: [Sc in each of next 5 sc, inc3 in next sc] 3 times. (24 sc)

ROUND 5: Working in **back loops** only, sc in each sc around. (24 sc)

ROUNDS 6-8: Working in both loops, sc in each sc around. (24 sc)

ROUND 9: [Sc in each of next 2 sc, sc-dec] around. (18 sc)

ROUND 10: Sc in each sc around. (18 sc)

ROUND 11: [Sc in next sc, sc-dec] around. (12 sc)

- Start stuffing Arm firmly, adding more as you go.

ROUNDS 12-17: Sc in each sc around. (12 sc)

ROUND 18: [Sc in next sc, sc-dec] 4 times. (8 sc)

ROUND 19: [Sc-dec] around. (4 sc) Fasten off leaving long tail for sewing.

- Using yarn needle and long tail, position Arms on either side of Neck at Round 1 and sew in place.

FEET (Make 2)

ROUNDS 1-4: Using Color A, repeat Rounds 1-4 of Arms. At the end of Round 4, there are 24 sc.

ROUND 5: [Sc in each of next 3 sc, inc in next sc] around. (30 sc)

ROUND 6: [Sc in each of next 4 sc, inc in next sc] around. (36 sc)

ROUND 7: [Sc in each of next 5 sc, inc in next sc] around. (42 sc)

ROUND 8: Working in **back loops** only, sc in each sc around. (42 sc)

ROUND 9: Working in both loops, sc in each sc around. (42 sc)

ROUND 10: [Sc in each of next 5 sc, sc-dec] around. (36 sc)

ROUNDS 11-12: Sc in each sc around. (36 sc)

ROUND 13: Sc in each of next 12 sc, [sc-dec] 6 times, sc in each of next 12 sc. (30 sc)

ROUND 14: Sc in each sc around. (30 sc)

- Start Stuffing Feet firmly, adding more as you go.

ROUND 15: [Sc in each of next 3 sc, sc-dec] around. (24 sc)

ROUND 16: Sc in each sc around. (24 sc)

ROUND 17: [Sc in each of next 2 sc, sc-dec] around. (18 sc)

ROUNDS 18-19: Sc in each sc around. (18 sc)

ROW 20: Fold last round flat and working through both thicknesses, sc in each of next 9 sc (to close the Foot). Fasten off leaving long tail for sewing to Body.

- Using yarn needle and long tail, position Feet on either side of Belly between Rows 5 & 12 and sew in place.

143

Designers

Dilek Yıldırım (Turkey) is a graduate of the faculty of Health Sciences from Gazi University. Most of her career was spent working with sick children, so she combined her passion for crochet with her love of children by making crochet toys for them. She is also a mother of three and after her children were born, she devoted more time to crochet and created a 'big world' with her own works and designs. She hosts a blog, called "dileksworld", where she shares her designs. At the same time she holds weekly Amigurumi courses for groups.

Katerina Nikolaidau (Greece) is married and mother to a wonderful daughter. She was about ten-years old when her loving grandmother taught her to crochet. Now, thirty-four years later, crochet is still a big part of Katerina's life. While experimenting with different crochet projects, she discovered the Japanese Amigurumi technique. After making her first Amigurumi doll, her passion for crocheting increased and soon she was designing her own patterns.

Kristi Tullus (Estonia) was looking for a unique gift for a baby shower, when she stumbled upon a few cute crocheted animals. She decided to try making them herself. After that, she made some more... Now, she can't seem to stop. She's been dabbling in amigurumi-making for the past five years and has learned a few things - mostly about how not to do things. Her mission these days is to share the useful knowledge she's gained about making crocheted toys.

Kristina Turner (USA) is a crochet designer specializing in cute amigurumi and crochet accessories. Her business, Tiny Curl, encourages crochet fun at any age with amigurumi patterns and ready-made crochet dolls and accessories. Kristina loves bright colors and takes inspiration from her three cats and watching cartoons.

Mari-Liis Lille (Estonia) is also known as "lilleliis" and has been crazy about amigurumi since 2008, when she first discovered crochet. Since then, the designing of toys has become her greatest passion and self-realization. Lilleliis patterns are known among true amigurumi fans all over the world.

Sandrine Deveze (France) uses yarn and thread to devise her own personal universe, filled with poetry and harmony. More than anything, she loves bringing these adorable, cuddly toys to life for her children and loved ones. She lives with her family in the Atlantic Pyrenees region. In 2009, she created her blog, "Tournicote...á cloche-pied".

✳ ✳ ✳

Soledad Iglesias Silva (Argentina) lives and works in Patagonia, in the valley of the province Rio Negro. Her mother taught her to crochet when she was nine years old, but it was only when she was expecting her third child that her passion for amigurumi awakened. Since then she has tried many different yarns and hooks and crocheted hundreds of dolls. Finally, she discovered that what she liked best was designing and creating new patterns. So, she started "Madelenón", named for her great-grandmother, also an avid crocheter.

Tatyana Korobkova (Russia) is from the Ukraine, but lives and works in Istanbul, Turkey. Even though she's designed about two hundred knitting patterns, she is best known for her sweet, amigurumi-style dolls and animals in either knit or crochet. Her designs bring together her love of yarn, skill of pattern writing, imagination and children's smiles.

Tine Nielsen (Denmark) always has yarn within her reach... Just the way she likes it. Yarn makes her happy, and she hopes this shines through in her designs. As the designer and founder of "Little Happy Crochet", she writes crochet patterns and books. Her designs are mostly stuffed animals, even though they sometimes don't look like real animals, but rather like animals that make her (and hopefully lots of children) happy.